DINERS, DRIVE-INS AND DIVES

Diners DRIVE-INS. DIVES

AN ALL-AMERICAN ROAD TRIP
...with Recipes!

 GUY FIERI | WITH ANN VOLKWEIN

WILLIAM MORROW
An Imprint of HarperCollinsPublishers

To my wife, Lori, and my sons, Hunter and Ryder

I could never do this without your love and support. It's for our benefit that I pursue this adventure, but you're also the ones who pay the greatest price when I'm away on the road.

To my friend and manager, Jack LaVer

So missed and so appreciated.

Finally, to my Mom and Dad

Thanks for encouraging me to think outside the box.

All photographs courtesy of the restaurants and Food Network except for page 43, by Warren Jagger; pages 46 and 48, by Cassie Jones; page 120, by Mike McKenzie, Hot Shots Imaging; and page 228, by Shiree Sanchez. Images on pages 3, 42, 82, 181, and 223 © 2008 Jupiterimages Corporation.

HarperCollins books may be purchased for educational, business, or sales promotional use. For information please write: Special Markets Department, HarperCollins Publishers, 10 East 53rd Street, New York, NY 10022.

Designed by Kris Tobiassen

Library of Congress Cataloging-in-Publication Data

Fieri, Guy.
    Diners, drive-ins and dives: an all-American road trip . . . with recipes/ Guy Fieri with Ann Volkwein.—1st ed.
        p. cm.
    Includes indexes.
    ISBN 978-0-06-172488-6
    1. Diners (Restaurants)—United States—Guidebooks. 2. Drive-in restaurants—United States—Guidebooks. 3. Restaurants—United States—Guidebooks. 4. Cookery, American. I. Volkwein, Ann. II. Title.
TX945.F4885 2008
647.9573—dc22   2008038638

12 ID/RRD 22

Contents

MIDWEST

WEST AND SOUTHWEST

Introduction

Several years ago, if somebody had told me I was going to win *Next Food Network Star* and do all of these shows, my dream show might've been, *What do Rock-and-Roll Bands Eat?* I didn't dream up *DD&D*, but when I was given the chance to come into these restaurant owners' lives and share them with America, that was truly a gift.

So this is how it came together: producer David Page is the creative genius who pitched *DD&D*, and Food Network recommended he try me out as host for a special. So, I canceled some events and flew out on a red-eye to this little diner—Bayway Diner in Linden, New Jersey. I stumble out of the limo like, "So, what's up, guys?" and David, Bunny, and Chico (see "Meet the Crew") looked at me like I was naked. I say, "What's this about, what are we going to shoot?" So they tell me to go in and ask these questions—like I'm going to listen. So I'm rockin' and rollin' and doing my thing. Twenty minutes go by and David pulls me outside and says, "What was that?" And I say, "I don't know, I thought I was doing what you wanted me to do." And he says, "Can you do that again?" And I say, "That? Yeah, that's what I do at my restaurants," and he goes, "Oh my god, this is going to be out of control." Talking about it now with Chico and Bunny, they say they were like, "Oh yeah, some jerk-off from California

with bleached hair and flip-flops is going to come and make television—we're dead. This is going to be a one-shot wonder." This show was their baby. (And Mike Guinta, the owner of the Bayway, has now become a friend of mine.)

The show is about capturing Americana, and it embodies what the food business is in the United States. Some of the greatest chains originally started as mom-and-pop restaurants. I'm a small-restaurant owner myself; I know their marketing budgets are small. So, to have a chance to recognize these family institutions, these cultural epicenters, is unbelievable. I'm more honored to be in their presence. They say thank you so much for coming, and I say thank you so much for existing, because this is what America is about, the opportunity and the cultural bridges.

I recently went back to six of the diners, more than a year after shooting. I got goosebumps listening to the stories about how their business has improved and the successes they've shared—I'm just going, you're kidding me! I don't think I could be more passionate about it.

We've visited and continue to visit some of the greatest places across the United States, and this book is just a very brief introduction to some of those great places.

1

HOW I GOT MY WHEELS

Check out our first special that we shot and you'll see that we used this very car, among others. Since at that point it was a one-shot deal, we didn't have any cars so the producer got creative and contacted local car clubs. Now I'm a big Chevy fan; I won't drive a Ford; I'll drive a Dodge if I have to. So this lady brings up this black on red '67 Supersport Camaro and it *really* needed some work. So when the show gets picked up and everything is going

Where's Guido?

great, I ask, "Well, what are we going to do for a car?" David says, "I bought one." So I said, "I hope you didn't buy . . . anything but that '67 . . . !" So we got the work done and of course it's a great car now.

THERE ARE SOME PEOPLE I'D LIKE TO THANK . . .

The funny thing about this is I'm just a dude that owns restaurants and loves people, likes to tell stories and to have a good time. I've got to be so clearly honest with you—it's the entire *DD&D* team that makes this work. There's close to thirty or forty people who pull this show off and they deserve huge accolades. I feel like we're astronauts exploring a new world and they're back on the phone lines getting flights, hotels, hard drives—it's 24/7, it's like Engine 51 calling the hospital (if you get my *Emergency!* 1970s TV show reference).

The David Page Productions team and crew is the best in the world. Special thanks to production assistant Drew Sondeland and associate producer Nick Guettler for chasing down facts, pictures, and more for this book.

Many thanks to Food Network president Brooke Johnson, production gurus Bob Tuschman, Allison Page, Jordan Harman, and Susie Fogelson and Amanda Melnick in marketing. And thanks to the truly awesome Food Network Kitchens team. For gathering and editing art, stories, and recipes: Susan Stockton, plus Ashley ("Triple A") Archer, Rupa Bhattacharya, Shirley Fan, Danielle LaRosa, Loan Nguyen, and Mory Thomas. Recipe testing: lead Miriam Garron and Morgan Bennison, Graciel Caces, Treva Chadwell, Leah Cooksey, Charlotte March, Andrea Parkins, Maryann Pomeranz, Marissa Zeolla. Recipe editing: Katherine Alford and Lynn Kearney.

Thanks to Jason Hodes and Jeff Googel at William Morris for their great guidance and representation.

And to HarperCollins: it's a wonderful thing to see *DD&D* take another step by spreading the written word on good Americana food. Many thanks to Lisa Gallagher, Cassie Jones, Johnathan Wilber, Dina Magaril, Kris Tobiassen, Lucy Albanese, Paula Szafranski, Joyce Wong, and Nyamekye Waliyaya.

Thanks to the Krew and Steve, Amy and all the team members at Johnny Garlic's and Tex Wasabi's.

And last, but by no means least, thank you to my writer and alter ego, Ann Volkwein, for pulling together my thoughts and words (kinda like herding cats) into this fabulous gastronomic tour of America's Triple D's. She rocks!

Take a Trip to Flavortown

One of my favorite one-liners is to look at a big tub of marinara or something simmering away and say, "That looks like a hot tub in Flavortown." It's nothing more than entertaining me or my crew, but it makes it into the show every so often, and people come up to me sometimes and say "So where is Flavortown?" If there were a whole town made of flavors, a big hamburger might be the steering wheel on the bus that's going to Flavortown—and that's happened, at a place called Hillbilly Hot Dogs in Lesage, West Virginia. I was the grand marshal of a NASCAR race one day and a dude walked up to me and said "I want to be the mayor of Flavortown!" I just about wet myself it was so funny. We may not have a mayor yet, but we've got a conductor on the train going to Flavortown at Tom's Bar-B-Q in Memphis, and Uncle Gus of the Marietta Diner in Marietta, Georgia, asked to be the driver of the bus going to Flavortown.

You got it, Uncle Gus.

Hitting the road in search of Flavortown has been quite a trip for my palate, too. See, I have a fiduciary responsibility (that's a big word for me by the way) to eat everything. I ate lambs' tongue the other day, turtle soup, bulls balls, gizzards—just not stuff I'm excited to eat sometimes. But if you go somewhere and gizzards are their thing, you gotta eat it.

Me and the number-one bus driver goin' to Flavortown. All aboard!

Meet the Crew

In my crew of buddies, everyone gets a nickname—and Triple D *is no different.
These people make the show so great, and I can't thank them enough.*

Me

GUY FIERI

NICKNAME: "Guido"
BACK STORY: Guido's always been mine. I have never had another; it always stuck. It's kinda funny because I'm from California with bleached blond hair and not what you'd expect with that nickname. My wife is from Rhode Island and jokes, "I come all the way from Rhode Island and end up marrying a guy named Guido." I'm so proud to be Italian, and it raises some eyebrows.

Producer

DAVID PAGE

NICKNAME: "Klinger"
BACK STORY: It's not just the look, I mean I know he's not wearing a dress, but it's also the craziness that begat his name. He's every bit Section Eight; the guy is wild—and top of his game, a true TV visionary.

Field Producers

BRYNA LEVIN

NICKNAME: "The Pirate"
BACK STORY: Bryna wears giant sun hats that look like pirate hats, *always* wears stripes, and can captain a ship/shoot as well as anyone.

KATE GIBSON

NICKNAME: "Ask Kate"
BACK STORY: Simply put, whenever there was a question on a shoot, the answer was "Ask Kate." So it became her nickname. I can't tell you how many people wondered if it was some new kind of name. . . .

MIKE MORRIS

NICKNAME: "Father Time"
BACK STORY: Because he has more experience than all of the road crew put together.

Shooters

ANTHONY RODRIGUEZ

NICKNAME: "Chico"
BACK STORY: It started as "Chico and the Man" because he reminded me of Freddie Prinz. And then "Chico and the Bunny" (see below) was such an easy way to reference these guys—Chico means "small" in Spanish, and compared to Bunny, who's huge, you've got little Anthony.

MATT GIOVINETTI

NICKNAME: "Beaver"
BACK STORY: The printable story is that his Buddhist ways are like *Leave It to Beaver*.

Sound

DAVID CANADA

NICKNAME: "Big Bunny"
BACK STORY: Because when he raises his headphones up high on his head and walks around with the boom, he looks like an enormous rabbit flopping around holding a carrot. He's a big guy, like six foot one.

CRAIG ALRECK

NICKNAME: "Arnie"
BACK STORY: Because he works out all the time, has a back the size of a Buick and arms like cannons. The story was when Craig first came on, I made mention that his calves looked like tree trunks, then I saw him in the gym one day and was like, "He makes me want to work out" . . . and it just grew from there.

Production Assistants

MARK FARRELL

NICKNAME: "Meltdown"
BACK STORY: On his first day on the job, he was driving me from San Jose to our location and I was on the phone and midway through the drive, Mark started beating his head against the steering wheel saying, "I'm fired, I'm fired, I screwed up, I'm fired." I asked what was the matter and he said, "I was supposed to grab the new monitor at the desk." So when I got to location I came up to Anthony and David and said, "This guy's having a meltdown." Turns out the monitor was not important, but it was a look into how much he cares about every little thing about the job.

NEIL MARTIN

NICKNAME: "Boy Band"
BACK STORY: This one is simply because he wears his beard real skinny along just his jawline, like any of the boy band members would . . . and because he poses in a boy band way in every picture.

A1 Diner

EST. 1946 (AS HEALD'S DINER), RE-EST. 1988 ★ THE GOURMET DINER ON STILTS

This diner in Maine is up on stilts, and the food is on another level, too. In 1946 the Worcester Lunch Car Company built diner number 790 and delivered it right here, to Gardiner, Maine. Now under its fourth owner, this local legend is serving up way more than traditional diner fare.

★ TRACK IT DOWN ★

**3 Bridge Street
Gardiner, ME 04345
207-582-4804
www.a1diner.com**

They've got the basics like eggs sunny-side up, chili dogs, or meatloaf with gravy, but then they've also got specials like Szechuan beef sauté, lamb tagine with couscous, or chicken Marbella. Co-owner Mike Giberson says you can blame that on Kenneth. Kenneth Harrison is a Seattle transplant who's given free reign by the owners to do what he's feelin' in the kitchen. (Being an owner myself, I can say this is a sweet deal.) He does a Greek flank steak roulade stuffed with garlic, spinach, marinated artichoke hearts, roasted red pepper, and feta. It's bananas. And as Kenneth notes, "Bananas is good."

The locals have responded well to the new dishes, and at a diner that's been running for sixty years, they've got some serious regulars. In revitalizing the diner they had to attract a younger clientele, plus they wanted to make the food they liked. Like mojito-glazed duck, for example. Kenneth lets the fresh mint leaves settle into the sugar that makes the rum glaze. We've all had moments when duck has gone wrong; but this is ducklicious.

But don't think they ignore the diner classics. Mike tells the waitstaff to get a menu into people's hands immediately, lest they think all the diner serves is mojito duck or Asian corn fritters. Among many other items, they make banana walnut pancakes; chicken pot pie with fresh, hand-pulled chicken, fresh veggies, sage, and a scratch-made crust; and some "money" biscuits whipped up by Bob Newell, the hashman who's been working here for more than half a century.

A1 DINER HISTORY

Originally the diner was named Heald's Diner, owned by Eddie Heald. After ordering it in Worcester at the factory (Eddie's daughter Marguerite remembered it was "top of the line"), they set it up on twenty-foot stilts next to the bridge over Cobbossee Stream in the center of town. He'd cut the front part of a former garage off to make room for it—thus the kitchen, in what's left of the building, is much larger than a normal diner's. The second owner was Maurice Wakefield, who bought the diner in 1952, renaming it Wakefield's. Maurice would run it for almost thirty years, totally dedicated to making real-deal pies and gravy for the workingman of Gardiner.

Mike Giberson's father, Albert, known as Gibey, was the diner's third owner, buying it in 1979 on a whim and renaming the diner Giberson's. His wife, Elizabeth, did the books and he did the cooking, soon hitting his stride making donuts at three AM and New England boiled dinners on Thursdays. When his thoughts turned to selling in the mid-eighties, he called his son Mike in LA, who promptly said he was coming home. Mike became the fourth owner of the diner in 1988, along with his partner, Neil Anderson. They met while working at Legal Seafood together in Boston. (Mike had been cooking, even in secret, since the age of ten.) They renamed the place A1, inspired by an A1 Neon sign that Neil had once given Mike, who is a big fan of neon. The art moderne interior, in mahogany, tiles, sunburst stainless steel, is all original, including the specials board. Mike says, "I can no longer buy the red letters [on the board]; those red letters are special to me."

Getting here was quite a trip. I take a flight to Maine, coming from the West Coast in my tank top and flip-flops. I think I had a T-shirt with me. . . . I get there and step into six inches of snow. I don't know what happened, but somehow I didn't have tennis shoes. So there I am at midnight in Maine and we have to drive thirty miles up to this place from the airport—but it took three and a half hours, it was snowing so bad. So I come walking into the lobby of this place in flip-flops, and they see me—they thought I just got off planet Pluto. Great people.

This diner is suspended twenty feet in the air (really!).

Mike's Maine Crab Cakes

ADAPTED FROM A RECIPE FROM *A1 DINER: REAL FOOD, RECIPES, AND RECOLLECTIONS*
BY SARAH ROLPH, TILBURY HOUSE PUBLISHERS, 2006

These are loaded with crab, and even in a state that is famous for this dish, people come to Gardiner to track them down.

MAKE 16 (3-OUNCE) CRAB CAKES

1½ pounds fresh crabmeat, picked over for shells

1½ cups fresh corn (or frozen corn, thawed)

¾ cup diced red bell pepper

¾ cup chopped celery

¾ cup finely chopped yellow onion

1½ cups mayonnaise

¾ teaspoon dry mustard

¾ teaspoon salt

½ teaspoon freshly ground black pepper

1 large egg, lightly beaten

2½ cups saltine cracker crumbs, divided

2 tablespoons unsalted butter, plus more as needed

SPECIALS
8 OZ ANGUS SIRLOIN W CHIPOTLE BUTTER 1395
COWBOY BEEF STEW   1275
GREEK BEEF STEW   1225
RUSSIAN VEGETABLE STRUDEL   1095
GREEK SALAD W FRIED CALAMARI   1075
WILD MUSHROOM RAGOUT   1095
FRESH FRIED HADDOCK   1250
MOUSSAKA   1195
2 PORK CHOPS W APPLE CHUTNEY   1350
MANICOTTI W MUSHROOMS & FENNEL   1095
RISOTTO W ASIAN CHICKEN   1250

1. Mix the crabmeat, corn, bell pepper, celery, onion, mayonnaise, and mustard in a medium bowl. Season with the salt and pepper. Gently fold in the beaten egg and 1½ cups of the cracker crumbs, taking care not to overwork the mixture.

2. Place the remaining 1 cup crumbs on a plate or in a shallow dish.

3. Form the crab mixture into 3-ounce patties, about 3 inches in diameter. Coat the cakes with the cracker crumbs, on both sides, by placing each cake in the dish of crumbs and pressing gently.

4. Heat a large skillet over medium-high heat, add the butter, and cook the crab cakes until golden brown, about 6 minutes per side. Serve.

Blue Moon Café

EST. 1996 ★ EAT COMFORT FOOD IN YOUR PJS

For a lot of folks, comfort food is breakfast. Here in Baltimore at the Blue Moon Café they're doing all the classics like eggs, French toast, and pancakes, but they're doing them their own way. Case in point: their Cap'n Crunch–encrusted French toast, or lox and cream cheese on homemade crepes instead of bagels.

There's something for everybody, and it's all made from

★ TRACK IT DOWN ★

1621 Aliceanna Street
Baltimore, MD 21321
410-522-3940

scratch. Make yourself at home; as one regular notes, "You could come here in your pajamas and I'm pretty sure they wouldn't care." The café actually is home to chef and owner Sarah Simington, who lives in the house upstairs. As she says, she's on top of things—literally. It's a natural fit; she was raised in her mom's restaurant, and it was her mom who found this place for rent. Sarah leapt at the chance, saying, "An opportunity like this comes around once in a blue moon." Her recipes come just as naturally: "Everything's made in my head, and I just play it out."

Like that French toast: she uses legit crunch of the Cap'n as her crust. That's got to be against the law if you're in the Cap'n Crunch club, but when you see how the sugar gets caramelized up and the Crunch stays crunchy, you'll see it's worth breaking the rules. She finishes it off with fresh whipped cream, blue-

When you see this sign, you know it's on like Donkey Kong!

She's like Bionic Woman fast—that, or my eyes are goin'!

berries, and more of the Crunch. The fruit's acidity balances the sweet, and the whipped cream acts like the milk.

She also makes a savory meat roll. It's kind of a cross between a cinnamon roll and a stromboli. She loads it with sausage, mozzarella, and a cashew-basil pesto with organic Parmesan and rolls it into a biscuit dough spiral. It's topped with sautéed peppers, mushrooms, onions, and tomatoes and served with a side of hash browns. If you look in the dictionary, I bet the definition of comfort food has a picture of that alongside.

From basics like biscuits and gravy to eggs Benny to a homemade green chili on huevos rancheros, every dish tastes like Mom made it—wherever your home is. And they're open late-night Friday and Saturday for the after-party crowd.

Cap'n Crunch French Toast

ADAPTED FROM A RECIPE COURTESY OF BLUE MOON CAFÉ

I know it's tough, but try not to eat all the cereal beforehand.

4 TO 5 SERVINGS

¾ **cup heavy cream**

3 **large eggs, lightly beaten**

2 **tablespoons sugar**

1 **teaspoon pure vanilla extract**

3 **cups Cap'n Crunch cereal**

8 **to 10 slices bread, such as Texas toast or French bread**

Butter for cooking

Topping

1 **cup heavy cream**

2 **tablespoons confectioners' sugar**

1 **teaspoon pure vanilla extract**

2 **cups assorted fresh seasonal berries**

No pajamas, no food?

1. Mix the cream, eggs, sugar, and vanilla in a large bowl and whisk until combined.

2. Put the cereal in a storage bag and use a rolling pin to crush cereal until it resembles cracker meal. Transfer the cereal to a shallow dish.

3. Dip a couple slices of the bread into the cream mixture until soft but not completely soaked. Let excess liquid drip from the bread, then press into the cereal crumbs to coat evenly. Place on a sheet pan and repeat with the remaining slices.

4. Heat a large skillet or griddle over medium heat, add butter as needed, and cook the bread until caramelized on both sides, about 6 to 8 minutes total.

5. For the whipped cream topping: Beat the cream, confectioners' sugar, and vanilla in a large bowl with a hand mixer to soft peaks. Dollop on top of the French toast and serve with the berries.

Oh, the Cap'n Crunch Club is gonna get you, missy!

Chap's Pit Beef

EST. 1987 ★ CARNIVORE HEAVEN OVER CHARCOAL

Arriving in Baltimore, we used the inside track of our buddy Duff Goldman of Charm City Cakes to find out one of his favorite joints. He said locals know you've got to get pit beef. So we headed to the famous Chap's for charcoal pit beef.

★ TRACK IT DOWN ★

**5801 Pulaski Highway
Baltimore, MD 21205**
410-483-2379
www.chapspitbeef.com

It started over twenty years ago when Bob and Donna Creager got married. As a wedding gift her father gave her "this little shack," as she puts it, and he thought since her new husband loved to cook they should put a pit beef stand here, outside his nightclub. "We started with just a grill, an exhaust system, and a register." But they learned real fast and brought in so many fans they had to add on a dining room. Done the way you want—rare, medium-well, whatever you like—the beef is then sliced thin and piled high.

They start the day placing six big bottom rounds straight on the 400- or 500-degree charcoal grill. Slap some white onions, bright, fresh horseradish, and a little salt and pepper on a roll (but not too big a roll, this is about the meat) and you're there. Wow!

The meat is so tender, with a nice charcoal edge, that locals give it way past a ten. They sell a couple hundred a day of those sandwiches, but they're putting way more than that on the pit. There's ham, turkey, sausage, and even corned beef for killer Reubens, and combos any way you

"Eat burgers!" "Eat cake!" The great debate.

The Carnivore Capital.

want. Bob's favorite is the Bulldog: he puts a couple slices of cheese on a roll, the sausage on top, and then the beef on top of that. Or try a combo of sweet ham, briny, pickley spiced corned beef, and smoky pit beef. It's a good mouthful.

I custom made a tower of a sandwich for my boy Duff, with beef, jalapeños, horseradish, ham, then a burger, cheese sauce, pickles, chopped beef, and turkey. It was pure cascading joy.

As one regular describes it, "It's like going over to a family member's house and they've got the grill out. Only they're always open and they don't mind you stoppin' by."

Bottom line, this is carnivore heaven.

Duff really wanted to drive, but I said, "You didn't let me bake a cake!"

#52 Sub Sandwich

ADAPTED FROM A RECIPE COURTESY OF CHAP'S PIT BEEF

This is the oven-roasted method, but if you can roast it over a charcoal fire it would be that much closer to Chap's.

MAKES 8 SANDWICHES

2 pounds beef bottom round

Kosher salt and freshly ground black pepper

2 tablespoons olive oil

Spice rub (optional)

8 sub rolls

1½ pounds sliced ham

1½ pounds sliced American cheese

1½ pounds sliced corned beef

Sliced onions

Prepared horseradish

1. Preheat the oven to 350°F.

2. Heat a large skillet over high heat. Season the beef all over with salt and pepper to taste. Add the oil to the pan, and then sear the beef on both sides, turning once, until a rich brown. Transfer the beef to a roasting pan and sprinkle with your favorite spice rub, if desired.

3. Put the beef in the oven and roast until a meat thermometer inserted in the thickest part of the meat registers 140 to 145°F. Set aside to cool.

4. To build the sandwiches: Thinly slice the beef, and layer in the rolls with the ham, cheese, and corned beef. Serve with the sliced onions and horseradish on the side.

J.T. Farnham's

EST. 1941, RE-EST. 1994 ★ LET THE FRESH FISH DO THE TALKIN'

....

★ TRACK IT DOWN ★

88 Eastern Avenue (Route 133)
South Essex, MA 01929
978-768-6643

They've been doing fried clams here for seventy years. That's right; this is the home of the whole-belly fried clam in Massachusetts. I stopped by here looking for a lobster roll, and also got fresh day scallops, haddock, and all kinds of fried seafood.

They don't just serve clam strips here but the whole deal, with the big belly-soft center that gives it loads of flavor. Clam strips are for city dwellers, the locals say. Joe and Terry Cellucci jumped at the chance to buy this place fourteen years ago, she a stay-at-home mom and he a high-tech guy. They were new to the restaurant game, but the lure was too strong for these locals to not return this place to its heyday one clam at a time.

The clams are dipped in evaporated milk whipped with a secret mixture. Then they are coated in plain and simple corn flour. No salt, no pepper. Joe and Terry say they're out just to get the seafood flavor. Once the extra flour is knocked off, the clams are fried in fresh hot oil, which is changed about every two hours to keep the clam taste clean and pure.

The number-one-selling item on the menu is the fisherman's combo. It's got it all: fish, scallops, clams, shrimp, onion rings, and fries. The scallops and fish are fried in one group, then shrimp and clams and the onion rings and fries. Joe likes to get the fry to just beyond the canary yellow, to a brownish stage.

Joe keeps an eye on the ordering and he keeps it fresh. His rule is to let the fish do the talking, as many ways as it can, from three types of chowder to steamed, fried, or grilled lobster.

This is the version of popcorn at the Fried Clam Movie Theater.

Aunt Nancy's Coleslaw

ADAPTED FROM A RECIPE COURTESY OF J.T. FARNHAM'S

Here's a real-deal coleslaw that's just sweet and sour enough to complement all that fry.

4 GENEROUS SERVINGS

1 (8-ounce) can chunk unsweetened pineapple,
    in juices, strained

1 carrot, peeled and roughly chopped

1 cup mayonnaise

⅓ cup sugar

2 teaspoons white wine vinegar

1 teaspoon celery seeds

1½ pounds green cabbage, shredded

Kosher salt

Freshly ground black pepper

1. Put the pineapple and carrots into a food processor and pulse until finely chopped.

2. Stir together the mayonnaise, sugar, vinegar, and celery seeds in a large bowl.

3. Add the cabbage and the pineapple-carrot mixture, and toss until evenly coated. Season to taste with salt and pepper.

4. This slaw is best if made several hours or the day before so the flavors can come together. Keep covered in the refrigerator until ready to serve.

"Mar–Nov"? Must be French for no shirt, no shoes . . . no dice. (Yeah, that works.)

Red Arrow Diner

EST. 1922 ★ HAVE A LANDMARK DINER DAY

Head to this eighty-five-year-old New Hampshire 24/7 go-to diner spot and stand in line. It's totally worth it. Owner Carol Sheehan grew up in the restaurant biz and has been keeping this place classic for twenty years.

★ TRACK IT DOWN ★

61 Lowell Street
Manchester, NH 03101
603-626-1118
www.redarrowdiner.com

They've got real home cooking that's heavy on the New England traditions like corned beef and cabbage and home-made baked beans and toast, or just plain old comfort food like open-faced fresh roast turkey with gravy or shepherd's pie. Every day of the week there's a different blue-plate special—actually served on a blue plate. For the past five years, Roy Donohue has been the chef de cuisine here, and he says his specialty is every single home-cooked dish in America. If you're there on a Wednesday, you too can discover a New England favorite: American Chop Suey. I'd never heard of it before. They were shocked. The whole restaurant was shocked. Roy says, "It's all-American hamburg with macaroni." He takes a heated pan and slaps some butter in there. Butter, not oil! He throws in the ground meat, then some onions to sauté in there, then green bell pepper, ground dried garlic, oregano, basil, and a can of tomato strips without juice. It's mixed up with cooked macaroni; as Roy says, "Sweet!" (Every time I would say something is nice, Roy would say "SWEEEEET!" Back and forth, back and forth—what a funny guy.)

The bean recipe here is from 1922 and includes brown sugar and molasses—also "sweet"—and he deep-fries his French toast. It's like close encounters of the Roy kind. Then there's something called a pork pie. It's Carol's grandmother's recipe done Roy style with ground pork, spices, and a poultry seasoning that's all whipped up with homemade mashed potatoes and baked with a fresh top crust. He takes as much care with his food as a grandmother would.

When it's time for dessert, Rachel McCullough steps in. She's been baking all her life, and it shows. She does it all, pies, cakes, and an original, home-baked twist on a particular clas-

THE RED ARROW DINER STORY

The original founder was David Lamontagne, who ran five Red Arrows throughout the city. Longtime employee Levi Letendre eventually bought the Red Arrow from the Lamontagnes and ran it until his retirement in 1978. His legacy endured through several owners up until today. Carol Sheehan purchased the diner in 1987 when it became vacant for the first time since 1922. Now landmarked by the city, this is the spot the politicians come by during primary season. Adam Sandler included it in his movie *Eight Crazy Nights*; and the Bare Naked Ladies were so impressed during a visit that they wrote a song about it, which plays every six minutes outside, along with another song written by Manchester's own Matt Farley. But that's got nothing on this book—ha ha ha.

sic packaged snack cake: the Twinkie. Around here they call them "Dinah fingers." A little yellow food coloring in the batter gives them that identifiable hue, and they're filled with a mixture that includes marshmallow spread, vanilla, and confectioners' sugar for a taste that's delicious and definitely homemade.

Come by any time. They're only closed sixteen hours a year, from 2 PM Christmas Eve to 6 AM Christmas morning—which turns into the busiest day of the year.

American Chop Suey

ADAPTED FROM A RECIPE COURTESY OF RED ARROW DINER

NOTE FROM THE OWNERS: Since we were on the Food Network, we have received thousands of e-mails wanting our recipe for American Chop Suey. Well, Carol has decided to unlock her recipe vault, so here you go!

SERVES 8

3 tablespoons butter

1 medium yellow onion, chopped

1 green bell pepper, stemmed, seeded, and chopped

2 garlic cloves, minced

1 pound ground beef

1 teaspoon dried oregano

1 teaspoon dried basil

½ teaspoon ground black pepper

Kosher salt

1 (14.5-ounce) can diced tomatoes

1 (14.5-ounce) can tomato sauce

¼ cup tomato paste

⅔ cup tomato juice

Pinch of sugar

1 pound elbow macaroni

1. Heat the butter in a large pot over medium heat. Add the onion and bell pepper and cook, stirring occasionally, until soft, about 5 minutes. Add the garlic and cook, stirring, for about 1 minute. Then add the ground beef and continue to cook, stirring and breaking up the chunks of meat with a spoon. Cook until the meat is no longer pink, about 7 minutes. Sprinkle the herbs and pepper over the meat, add salt to taste, and mix in well.

2. Add the canned tomatoes with their juices, the tomato sauce, paste, and juice. Add sugar to taste. Simmer while you cook the pasta.

3. Bring a large pot of salted water to a boil over high heat. Add the macaroni and cook, stirring occasionally, until al dente. Drain. Mix the macaroni into the chop suey. Serve hot.

Cruisin' in da '67 . . . so *sweeeeet* . . . nice . . . ! Just like Roy would say.

Bayway Diner

EST. 2005 ★ THE FIRST PLACE WE SHOT, WHERE IT ALL BEGAN

When it comes to classic American road food, nobody does it better than New Jersey. I mean, they've got more diners than any other state. Check this one out and you'll see that you don't have to be big to be "big."

They've got nine seats at the Bayway, but they serve 250 people a day. It's a zoo. They serve big plates to big crowds of big guys. The diner sits right across the street from one of the country's biggest refineries and a few miles from the port of Newark. Owner Mike Guinta says, "That's what we're here for, grab an egg and bacon sandwich and a coffee and go to work . . . There ain't no mochaccino here. You give them a good sandwich for a good price and they're coming back." Regulars say it's all made with love and better than Mom's.

Their Bayway Monster Burgers are two 8-ounce patties strong with Taylor ham, lettuce, and tomato, and they'll add cheese and bacon if you want. Mike grew up in diners and he says he needs to have everything the best. But he'd never run a diner or any restaurant before. He's a fireman by trade and runs a garbage business around the corner. It all came about when he needed a place for a garage and they thought they'd knock this old diner down and put the garage here. But they just couldn't do it. "We said, you know what? There's not that many good places to eat around here." So they rebuilt the diner for themselves.

"Hey, stylist, can ya make my hair like Guido's?"

Warning: the Bayway Diner does not have real monsters . . .

After fifty years the diner was a mess, so they had to shut it down temporarily and restorer Randy Garbin spent two and a half months refurbishing it. And man does this place scream diner, from the shining siding to the Bayway clock above the door. "It's my passion," explains Mike. "When I do something, I try to do it to perfect." Including hiring Joe Gonzalez as a short-order cook—but he's really a short-order chef. He serves up food you wouldn't expect in a diner, like Cajun-grilled chicken marinated overnight and served over tri-color pasta or a made-from-scratch Philly cheesesteak. He starts with a twenty-two-pound top round that he bones, rolls, and ties himself and marinates with chicken base overnight. He then oven-roasts it with celery, onions, and carrots for two and a half hours. After it's cool, he slices it thin. That's some special meat for a cheesesteak.

At Bayway they're busy keeping the workingman happy, but everyone's welcome; just pull up next to the Vatco and come on in.

BAYWAY NEWS

Since the show aired, Mike's opened up a sister diner and put on his first Ms. Bayway Contest, and he's begun the tradition of a summertime luau, a clambake with an Elvis appearance, and an end-of-summer (Labor Day) C-Ya Party. They've now got a tent that seats an additional twenty-four to thirty people, but the place still gets packed.

Joe's Famous Tri-Color Pasta with Grilled Chicken

ADAPTED FROM A RECIPE COURTESY OF BAYWAY DINER

People line up for this dish that Chef Gonzalez serves with a smile.

SERVES 6

Chicken

⅔ cup white vinegar

½ cup crushed canned tomatoes

¼ cup extra-virgin olive oil

2 teaspoons kosher salt

1 teaspoon freshly ground black pepper

1 teaspoon dried parsley, or more, to taste

1 teaspoon dried oregano, or more, to taste

6 (4-ounce) boneless, skinless chicken breasts, butterflied

Pasta

1 pound tri-colored fusilli pasta

1 red bell pepper, stemmed, seeded, and finely diced

1 green bell pepper, stemmed, seeded, and finely diced

1 yellow bell pepper, stemmed, seeded, and finely diced

4 medium tomatoes, chopped

2 carrots, chopped

1 medium red onion, chopped

½ cup black olives, drained, pitted, and chopped

⅔ cup extra-virgin olive oil

⅔ cup red wine vinegar

¼ cup sugar

Kosher salt and freshly ground black pepper

3 tablespoons chopped fresh flat-leaf parsley, for garnish

1. For the chicken: Whisk the vinegar, tomatoes, olive oil, salt, pepper, and 1 teaspoon each of the parsley and oregano together in a large bowl. Add the chicken to the marinade, turning to coat evenly. Cover, and refrigerate for 2 to 3 hours.

2. Meanwhile, prepare the pasta: Bring a large pot of salted water to a boil over high heat. Add the pasta and cook, stirring occasionally, until al dente. Drain and cool.

3. Stir the bell peppers, tomatoes, carrots, onion, and olives together in a large bowl. In another bowl, whisk the oil, vinegar, and sugar together and season with salt and pepper to taste. Pour the dressing over the vegetables and season with salt and pepper. Add the pasta and toss to combine.

4. When ready to serve: Preheat a grill to medium-high heat.

5. Remove the chicken from the marinade, letting the excess liquid fall back into the bowl. Discard the marinade. Pat the chicken dry and place on the grill and cook, turning once, until cooked through but not dry. Cut the chicken into bite-size pieces.

6. Divide the pasta evenly among 6 plates and top with the chicken. Sprinkle on the chopped fresh parsley and serve.

The beginning of the Triple D whirlwind.

Brownstone Diner and Pancake Factory

EST. EARLY 1970S ★ THE HOUSE OF SHORT STACKS AND THE SPICY BUFFALO PANCAKE

You can find an average pancake just about anywhere, but finding a really killer pancake is a whole other deal. This family-owned joint in Jersey City is doing it right, thirty-one ways.

This family has been keeping tradition going for more than forty years. The first generation came from Greece, and the kids, Zoe, Maria, and Bobby, are now running it. All of them started out working in different professions, but they couldn't stay away. And do folks ever line up.

They make monster amounts of buttermilk batter fresh every day—and they hide their secret ingredient in their confectioners' sugar. The batter's nice and thick. Bobby Bournias showed me how to make honky tonk and nut 'n' honey pancakes off their menu of thirty-one different pancakes. He pours the batter and lets it sit for a little before adding the toppings. He first puts fresh-cooked crumbled bacon on one pancake, peanut butter chips on another—these are both for the honky tonk, it turns out. For the nut 'n' honey, he sprinkles almonds and walnuts on top, with a swirl of honey and a bit of powdered sugar right at the end. I would order that again. The honky tonk stack ends with a sliced banana served on top, and the peanut flavor shines through. They also do one with hot strawberry preserves served on top, with cool sour cream dolloped on with fresh strawberries. That is like warm, adult strawberry short cake. I think I shocked Bobby by ordering hot sauce and ketchup on my meat pancake, but that's what I'm talkin' about—it's good. They also do pancake wraps, which are like oversized pancakes with all sorts of good stuff inside. It's pigs in a blanket gone wild, like with eggs, potatoes, sausage, and cheese; those are some good

★ TRACK IT DOWN ★

**426 Jersey Avenue
Jersey City, NJ 07302
201-433-0471
www.brownstonediner.com**

savory pancakes. So I decided to make one northern-California style. My parents encouraged me to play with my food. I added breaded chicken with hot sauce, roasted pepper, and blue cheese on top. I swear, a spicy Buffalo pancake will sell—off da hook!

The dad, Peter Bournias, is famous around here for cooking up the family favorites from back in Greece. He makes moussaka for the gods, starting with sautéing some diced onion, a little parsley in olive oil, then a little white wine. The ground beef is added next and gets cooked down, then some diced tomatoes and a sprinkle of flour go in. Next he fries up some sliced potatoes and roasts sliced, skinned eggplant slices that are drizzled with olive oil.

You then layer all of the above like a Greek lasagna—potatoes, then eggplant, then meat—all topped off with a scratch-made béchamel sauce before baking it off. It's creamy, rich, and very popular. And I thought it was just a pancake factory—not that there's anything wrong with that—all day long.

The kids work long hours. Zoe loves the fact that she gets to scream all day, and she couldn't be happier, but she agrees with Maria that her parents should've had more kids, to split the shifts a little better.

Beaver moves so fast that he's blurry.

Nut 'n' Honey Pancakes

ADAPTED FROM A RECIPE COURTESY OF BROWNSTONE DINER AND PANCAKE FACTORY

Even without the secret ingredient, these are thick and rich and worth the effort.

SERVES 4 TO 5 (16 TO 20 PANCAKES)

2 cups buttermilk

1 cup vegetable oil

3 large eggs

1½ teaspoons vanilla syrup or vanilla extract

2 cups baking mix, such as Bisquick

2 teaspoons confectioners' sugar, plus more for garnish

2 teaspoons granulated sugar

¼ teaspoon baking powder

½ cup chopped slivered almonds

Butter

½ cup chopped pecans

½ cup chopped walnuts

Honey

"How many in yer party? My sister will seat you after she eats her toy."

1. Combine the buttermilk, oil, eggs, and vanilla syrup in a large mixing bowl and whisk until fully incorporated. Whisk the dry ingredients (excluding the nuts) together in another bowl. Add the dry ingredients to the wet ingredients and mix until just combined. A few lumps here and there keep the pancakes fluffier.

Big smiles about great pancakes.

2. Heat the griddle until hot and brush with butter. Ladle out ¼ cup batter to make 4-inch-diameter pancakes. Mix the nuts together. After about 15 seconds, sprinkle a handful of the medley into the center of each pancake. Depending on the temperature of the griddle, after 30 seconds to a minute, the edges of the pancake should begin to curl. Using a spatula, flip the pancake over. After another 30 seconds or so, the pancake should be a light golden brown and can be removed from the griddle.

3. To finish off, drizzle honey over the pancakes and lightly dust with confectioners' sugar. Butter can be added to taste, although it's generally not needed since the pancakes should be very moist. To maintain fluffiness, the pancake batter should generally be used on the same day it is prepared.

We're in a kitchen, not a bathroom.

White Manna

EST. 1939 ★ TINY DINER, BIG-TASTING SLIDERS

This is a tiny burger joint with tiny burgers that brings in huge crowds. I could eat eighteen or seventy-five of these babies.

★ TRACK IT DOWN ★

**358 River Street
Hackensack, NJ 07601
201-342-0914**

They've been cranking out these tiny sliders for more than sixty years. Ronny Cohen and his brother bought the place in 1986 after moving here from Israel, and they kept almost everything just the way it was. Here at the White Manna the beef is never frozen—chopped beef is delivered every morning—and the burgers never sit under a heat lamp; they're cooked right in front of you. Grab a seat at one of the twenty stools that form a "U" around the grill or take a place in line outside. They "roll" around eight hundred to a thousand patties every day at this little red and white diner that's as cool as its miniature burgers.

What in the beginning was a business to Ronny soon became like a family. "You've got to love it," he says. "It's fun to work here." He says everything in this town could change over the years, but you'll always recognize the White Manna. They're dedicated to keeping it real.

Bursting with burgers.

SANDWICHES

HAMBURGER 110
CHEESEBURGER 130
DOUBLE HAMBURGER 180
DOUBLE CHEESEBURGER 205
STEAK & CHEESE 375

CHEESE SANDWICH 200
FRENCH FRIES 195 W—CHEESE 295

WITH LETTUCE & TOMATOES
50¢ EXTRA

50 0

DRINKS

SM 130   MD 160   LG 185

COCA COLA
DIET COKE
DR PEPPER
ROOT BEER
SPRITE
HI-C FRUIT PUNCH

UNSWEETENED ICED TEA
BOTTLED WATER
COFFEE & TEA
HOT CHOCOLATE

I wish gas prices were this low.

White Manna Burger

ADAPTED FROM A RECIPE COURTESY OF KELLY COHEN OF WHITE MANNA

Follow this road map for the best mini-sliders you'll ever eat. Every step's important, from the paper-thin Spanish onion to the Martin's potato rolls.

MAKES 8 MINI-BURGERS; SERVES 4

1 pound freshly ground lean beef

1 large Spanish onion, thinly sliced into half moons

8 slices American cheese

8 mini potato rolls (Martin's are great, www.potatoroll.com)

Ketchup

8 pickle slices

Mayonnaise, hot sauce, lettuce, and tomato, as desired

1. Heat a large cast-iron skillet over medium-high heat. (Do this while you form the burgers so it's good and hot.)

2. Divide the beef into 8 small balls, about 2 ounces each. Take care not to overwork the meat or the final burgers will be dense and tough. Put the burgers in the skillet (no oil needed) and scatter the onions on top. Use a spatula to smoosh the meat into a burger shape. When the burgers are brown, about 2 minutes, flip to cook the other side. Top with American cheese and cook until it is melted.

3. Place the burgers on the mini rolls and top with ketchup and pickles. Serve with mayonnaise, hot sauce, lettuce, and tomato, if desired.

Just add the apple pie and this is all–American.

Tick Tock Diner

EST. 1948 ★ EAT HEAVY

★ TRACK IT DOWN ★

**281 Allwood Road
Clifton, NJ 07012
973-777-0511
www.ticktockdiner.com**

The sign says it all at the Tick Tock. EAT HEAVY. It's 24/7 with this family, with one of the three boys there around the clock.

Frank and Jimmy took over the place from their dad, and George married into the business. Together they turn out diner classics that are as all-American as you can get, but get this: the chef is British-born Julian Clauss-Ehlers, and he's responsible for keeping the food real. He says, "We crack a thousand eggs daily. Every egg we cook is cracked to order." The chicken parm is made from scratch; there's fresh challah bread for the Monte Cristo sandwich; their grilled bacon, tomato, and cheese sandwich is called a "happy waitress"; and a huge local favorite is their "disco fries." As one regular says, "It's like a disco on your plate: brown gravy, mozzarella cheese, and fries." I get why they call it "disco fries": "heart attack fries" must've already been taken. Ha ha ha.

But Chef Julian's also serving up some dishes you might not expect, like chicken with portobello mushrooms flamed in brandy and finished with a little butter and parsley. Or check out his Cajun shrimp: sautéed with some red and yellow bell peppers and onion, house-made Cajun spice, chablis, house tomato sauce, and a little chicken stock. Delicious. The Tick Tock emphasizes freshness.

They might want to change the sign out front. EAT HEAVY AND GOURMET.

THE DINER COAST

West of the Rockies you have coffee shops, but diners on the East Coast are really melting pots of food. Tick Tock is a don't-miss example of this in all its glory.

Is that a scale or a clock between *eat* and *heavy*?

Veal Meatloaf

ADAPTED FROM A RECIPE COURTESY OF TICK TOCK DINER

This is classic comfort food, the kind every great diner should serve.

SERVES 6 TO 8

2 pounds ground veal

2 cups panko (Japanese-style bread crumbs, available at most markets)

½ yellow onion, finely diced

1 small red bell pepper, stemmed, seeded, and finely diced

1 small green bell pepper, stemmed, seeded, and finely diced

½ cup heavy cream

¼ cup grated Parmesan cheese

2 large eggs

3 tablespoons Dijon mustard

3 tablespoons ketchup

2 tablespoons Worcestershire sauce

1 tablespoon chopped fresh parsley

2 teaspoons dried herbes de Provence

2 teaspoons kosher salt

Freshly ground black pepper

1. Position an oven rack in the middle of the oven and preheat the oven to 350°F.

2. Mix all the ingredients together in a large bowl until completely incorporated. Spray a 9 by 13-inch baking dish with pan spray and form a loaf in the center. Spray the top of the loaf and cover with a piece of parchment paper. Bake for 25 minutes, then remove the parchment and continue cooking until cooked through, about 45 minutes. The juice should run clear when the meatloaf is poked, or look for an internal temperature of 150°F on an instant-read thermometer.

3. Let rest for 10 minutes before serving.

They have lots of reasons to smile at Tick Tock.

Eveready Diner

EST. 1972 ★ THE TAJ MAHAL OF DINERS

★ TRACK IT DOWN ★

4189 Albany Post Road
Route 9 North
Hyde Park, NY 12538
845-229-8100
www.theevereadydiner.com

You know when you're lucky enough to find a place that bakes their own pies, cakes, and breads it's usually a mom-and-pop joint. This diner is the major exception to that rule. The Eveready is huge and serves up to a thousand people a day, and the guys who run it keep it in the family: Uncle Teddy Vanikiotis, his sons Tommy and Costa, and their cousin Alex Serroukas. As Alex says, "It just doesn't taste as good if it isn't homemade." So, it's all homemade—from cheesecake to focaccia—in Uncle Teddy's bakery in the basement. They even make their own bread crumbs and coat their mozzarella sticks by hand.

They haven't changed their made-from-scratch ways since Uncle Teddy and his brother-in-law, who came over from Greece, opened a thirty-seat diner in 1972. In 1985 they tore down the original and put up this one, with three hundred seats.

Their pancake batter is an example of the care that goes into each recipe. It's not three-ingredient; it's got flour, milk, buttermilk, eggs, brown and white sugar, vanilla powder, and some malted milk. They serve the pancakes with fresh strawberry butter, and you can get your stack with hot flambéed apples from the family's own orchards.

GUY ASIDE

This is probably the Taj Mahal of diners. The bakery at this place will put the average bakery to shame. They've even got a bar; nothing wrong with that. Matter of fact, that is *bonus* points.

Another great handed-down, classic diner dish is the short ribs. Alex first rubs the ribs with salt and pepper and a mixture of fresh rosemary, thyme, and sage, then dredges them in flour before searing. Celery, carrots, onion, and fennel are chopped and sautéed, then the sauté pan is deglazed with red wine and the ribs and vegetables are placed in a roasting pan with some brown sauce and San Marzano canned tomatoes. Alex then covers the pan in foil and roasts the ribs for three hours covered, one hour uncovered. That's capital-T tender. It'll make your belly feel good.

Now about that bakery in the basement: it's like Teddy's art studio. He makes chocolate cakes; carrot cake; cheesecake; coconut custard, pecan, apple, banana cream, cherry, blueberry, and lemon meringue pies; and more than a dozen varieties of bread, from feta-olive-onion focaccia to pecan-cranberry-honey bread and panini bread. Most places buy their desserts, bread, and rolls. Teddy's philosophy for thirty-five years has been, "Who wants to eat the same bread and cakes every day?" He gives them variety and they keep coming back.

So come visit; you can't miss it. As Alex says, "It's an institution, man, it glows. It's like Vegas."

Earthquake drill. . . . Everyone's under the tables. . . . "It's safe to come out now."

Lobster Quesadillas

ADAPTED FROM A RECIPE COURTESY OF COSTA VANIKIOTIS, EVEREADY DINER

Half moons of cheesy goodness, these upscale quesadillas bring lobster into the fold with a shot of hot sauce.

MAKES 10 QUESADILLAS

1 small red onion, cut in chunks

2 plum tomatoes, halved

Salt and freshly ground black pepper

3 (8-ounce) packages cream cheese, softened

12 ounces coarsely grated Cheddar cheese

1 small bunch of scallions (white and green parts), chopped

3 tablespoons sriracha (Thai hot sauce, available at most markets)

Juice of 1 lime

10 (8-inch) flour tortillas

2 pounds cooked lobster meat, fresh or thawed frozen, sliced

2 tablespoons canola or olive oil, plus more as needed

Salsa, guacamole, and sour cream, for serving

1. Preheat the oven to 400°F. Put the chunks of onion and the tomato halves on a lightly oiled rimmed baking sheet, season with salt and pepper to taste, and roast until soft, about 15 minutes. Cool and coarsely chop the vegetables.

2. In a stand mixer with the paddle attachment, beat the vegetables, cream cheese, Cheddar, scallions, sriracha, and lime juice together on medium speed. Season with salt.

3. Place a tortilla on a work surface and spread ½ cup of the cheese mixture and 3 ounces of lobster evenly on half of the tortilla. Fold the tortilla over to make a half-moon-shaped quesadilla. Repeat with the remaining tortillas and filling.

4. Heat a large skillet over medium heat, add the oil and pan-fry the quesadillas, in batches, until brown and crispy, about 3 minutes per side. Cut into wedges and serve with salsa, guacamole, and sour cream.

Three-Cheese Macaroni and Cheese

ADAPTED FROM A RECIPE COURTESY OF COSTA VANIKIOTIS

Three types of cheese and super-crunchy panko bread crumbs make up this crazy-good mac.

4 TO 6 SERVINGS

1 tablespoon kosher salt, plus more for the pasta water

1 pound elbow macaroni

6 tablespoons (¾ stick) unsalted butter

6 tablespoons all-purpose flour

3 cups cold milk

1 cup heavy cream

1 pound white Cheddar cheese, shredded

4 ounces Romano cheese, shredded

4 ounces Asiago cheese, shredded

1 tablespoon freshly ground black pepper

2 cups panko (Japanese-style bread crumbs, available at most markets)

2 tablespoons chopped fresh flat-leaf parsley, for garnish

1. Preheat the oven to 325°F.

2. Bring a large pot of salted water to a boil over high heat. Add the macaroni and cook, stirring occasionally, until al dente, about 8 minutes. Drain.

3. Melt the butter in a large saucepan over medium heat. Sprinkle the flour over the butter and cook, whisking to make a paste (or roux), about 2 minutes. Add the milk and whisk vigorously until smooth. Reduce the heat to medium-low and cook, whisking occasionally, until the sauce is thick and bubbly. Add the heavy cream, all three cheeses, the 1 tablespoon salt, and the pepper. Cook, stirring, until the cheeses are fully melted.

4. Add the cooked macaroni to the cheese sauce and mix thoroughly. Transfer to a 9 by 13-inch baking dish and top with the panko crumbs. Bake the macaroni and cheese until hot and golden brown, about 15 minutes. Top with the fresh parsley. Serve.

MoGridder's

EST. 2006 ★ LOW AND SLOW BRISKET—AND AN OIL CHANGE

★ TRACK IT DOWN ★

**565 Hunts Point Avenue
Bronx, NY 10474
718-991-3046
www.mogridder.com**

*And check out his
new location in the
Arthur Avenue section at*

**632 E. 186th Street
Bronx, NY 10458**

Just to prove we'll go anywhere, we found this place stuck in the parking lot of an auto-repair shop in "da Bronx." From inside this thirty-five-foot trailer they're making barbecue that makes you feel like you're in Memphis. They've got brisket, ribs, pulled pork, and chicken that's slow-cooked in a massive smoker.

As one customer puts it, "Only in the Bronx can you watch your truck get a front windshield and eat some mean barbecue ribs out here." You can get a tune-up and some ribs, or how about a special of the day? Ribs, oil, and filter for $34.95.

Auto-shop owner Fred Donnelly didn't have any restaurant experience when he started. Barbecue was his hobby, and he used to bring in samples for the customers. He ended up with a barbecue truck and a dining room where a service bay used to be.

He does a dry rub with his spare ribs that's got salt, pepper, garlic, paprika, and a few things he won't give up. He also dry-rubs the brisket, then cooks it at 225°F for about ten hours using apple and cherry wood from the New Jersey

The USS MoGridder's BBQ Enterprise.

suburbs. The chicken is coated with olive oil, salt, and pepper before smoking, and it's served with a barbecue-sauce glaze. Everything cooks for a different amount of time. Badda bing. Low and slow, baby.

And the name? MoGridder was a childhood nickname his cousin slapped on him. No one knows what a MoGridder really is. So come to the corner of Hunts Point and Randall, where they do about a hundred fifty to two hundred lunches a day out of a monster rig at an auto shop. This is culinary dive 101 in the world of dives. They also do about thirty to forty windshields here a day, but Fred promises, "It's not a problem; you won't taste it."

Pork Butt

ADAPTED FROM A RECIPE COURTESY OF MOGRIDDER'S

This pork butt makes a mean pulled pork sandwich.

SERVES 6 TO 8

1 family-size pork butt
Salt
Granulated garlic
Freshly ground black pepper
MoGridder's Dry Rub Barbecue Seasoning (see page 49)
MoGridder's Barbecue Sauce (see page 49), for serving

Special equipment: oak, pecan, and fruit wood (apple or cherry), 4 pieces total

1. Season the pork butt (in this order!) with salt, granulated garlic, black pepper, and MoGridder's Dry Rub Barbecue Seasoning. Smoke the pork in a smoker at 220° to 225°F for 10½ hours or until fork tender.

2. Remove from the smoker and chop the meat. Serve with MoGridder's Barbecue Sauce.

Beef Brisket

ADAPTED FROM A RECIPE COURTESY OF MOGRIDDER'S

It's all about the right wood and a long smoking time.

SERVES 6 TO 8

1 family-size beef brisket

Granulated garlic

Freshly ground black pepper

MoGridder's Dry Rub Barbecue Seasoning (recipe follows)

MoGridder's Barbecue Sauce (see page 49), for serving

Special equipment: **oak, pecan, and fruit wood (apple or cherry), 4 pieces total**

1. Season the beef brisket with the granulated garlic, black pepper, and MoGridder's Dry Rub Barbecue Seasoning. Smoke the brisket in a smoker at 220° to 225°F for 6½ to 7 hours.

2. Remove from the smoker and slice the meat. Serve with MoGridder's Barbecue Sauce.

Just what you'd expect in an auto shop . . . where's the 10-W-40?

MoGridder's Dry Rub Barbecue Seasoning

Always store your seasonings out of the sunlight. I always make a double or triple batch, but be sure to do the math. (The granulated garlic slightly increases the flavor and makes the seasoning mixture sprinkle or shake better. Garlic powder can be used as a replacement.)

MAKES ABOUT 1 CUP

2½ tablespoons paprika

2 tablespoons kosher salt

2 tablespoons granulated garlic

2 tablespoons granulated sugar

1 tablespoon raw or granulated brown sugar

1 tablespoon chili powder

1 tablespoon freshly ground black pepper

1 tablespoon onion powder

1 teaspoon cayenne pepper

1 teaspoon dried oregano

1 teaspoon dried thyme

1. Mix everything together in a small bowl. Store in a glass jar with an airtight seal.

MoGridder's Barbecue Sauce

MAKES ABOUT 3½ CUPS

½ cup granulated sugar

1 teaspoon ground oregano

½ teaspoon dried thyme

1 teaspoon granulated garlic

2 teaspoons kosher salt (or to taste)

2 to 3 teaspoons freshly ground black pepper

½ cup white vinegar

1 cup molasses

1 cup ketchup

¾ cup prepared mustard

½ to 1 teaspoon cayenne pepper (optional)

1. Combine the first six ingredients in a medium nonreactive saucepan. Stir in enough vinegar to make a loose paste. Combine the remaining ingredients, incorporate well, and bring to a boil, stirring constantly. Reduce heat and simmer until thick, about 20 minutes.

The Dining Car

EST. 1961 ★ A GREAT AMERICAN DINER

At this Philly joint they've got it all . . . at any hour. Local favorites include chicken croquettes, pot roast, cinnamon French toast, and homemade bagels. Founder Joe Morozin Sr. lays it down: "If a customer wants to come here, day or night, he knows he can come to The Dining Car. . . . This diner's sure going to take care of you." He's been running restaurants for years and bought the original Dining Car in 1961. Almost twenty years later he replaced it with one right next door. Now it's run by his three kids, Nancy, Joe Jr., and Judy. Nancy recalls when they made the transition from one diner to the other, a lot of the customers "came in at six AM because they wanted to be the last one to eat at the old diner and the first one to eat in the new one." Some customers simply walked over to the new diner carrying their coffee cup with them.

★ **TRACK IT DOWN** ★

8826 Frankford Avenue
Philadelphia, PA 19136
215-338-5113
www.thediningcar.com

THE CAR

Built by the Swingle Dines company, The Dining Car is an homage to art deco, decked in silver and black with deco glass in sunburst designs, beveled mirrors, black enamel, stainless steel, glass block, and neon. As the owners say, with its rolled-top stainless-steel roof and long, sleek black body, you can almost find yourself looking for the rest of the train.

Chef Larry Thum has been at The Dining Car for more than thirty-three years. He started out as a dishwasher in high school and worked his way through the positions until he was head chef. Running a totally scratch kitchen (he even makes his own maple syrup), Chef Larry prepares classics like chipped beef that hark back to the 1940s. When I was a kid, my dad talked about having it in the navy, but this was a first for me. Larry mixes hot oil and flour so it makes a sort of paste (he says it can be like napalm if it gets on your skin), then he pours hot milk into the roux, which usually thickens

My son Hunter skateboarded
all over these sidewalks.

almost immediately. The cooked top round meat is sliced thin and chopped into squares. It's then "frizzled up" in a pan with some more hot oil before it's added to the gravy and then spooned over triangles of white toast. He sells seventy to eighty gallons of it a week. It's gotten a bad rap, but not when it's made here.

Being a part of *Diners, Drive-ins and Dives* has reconnected us to the community . . . and broadened our customer base, reminding them and us why we are here. The show helped us re-establish both our sense of purpose and our pride.

—THE MOROZIN FAMILY, THE DINING CAR

Then there's the deep-fried pork scraps and cornmeal called scrapple. The locals love to talk you into eating it. One of the diner's philosophies is to have a varied menu with a little bit for everybody. Crepes are also big here, after catching on a little bit at a time. The cooks make a crepe florentine filled with baked ham, Cheddar cheese, and spinach, with supreme sauce and mushrooms on top: welcome to comfort crepe.

Chicken Croquettes

ADAPTED FROM A RECIPE COURTESY OF CHEF LARRY THUM OF THE DINING CAR

Chef Larry says, "This is a very old traditional diner item. Years ago people used to take the scraps from their chicken, roll it up, bread it and fry it up, and get an extra meal out of it." It's like a diner dumpling; they make it into a cone, place it on a bed of mashed potatoes, and sauce it with a gravy of milk, chicken stock, and parsley. It's rich and big, and the sauce brings it home.

MAKES 14 CROQUETTES

Croquette Batter

1 cup milk

1 cup fresh chicken stock or canned broth

2 teaspoons freshly chopped flat-leaf parsley leaves

¼ teaspoon white pepper

Salt (only if using fresh chicken stock)

8 tablespoons (1 stick) unsalted butter

1 celery stalk, minced

1 cup all-purpose flour

1¼ pounds chicken meat, cooked and ground in a food processor

Breading

2 large eggs

2 cups milk

⅛ teaspoon kosher salt

3 cups all-purpose flour or cracker meal

3 cups bread crumbs

Chicken Gravy

3 tablespoons unsalted butter

3 tablespoons all-purpose flour

2 cups fresh chicken stock or canned broth

2 teaspoons chopped fresh flat-leaf parsley leaves

Pinch of salt and white pepper

Oil, for frying

Serving suggestion: mashed potatoes

1. For the croquette batter: Heat the milk and chicken stock in a heavy-bottomed saucepan over medium heat, and season with the parsley, white pepper, and salt (if using). Melt the butter in another saucepan over medium heat and add the celery; cook until slightly softened, about 2 minutes. Add the flour to the butter and celery and cook, stirring, to make a paste (or roux), about 3 minutes. Gradually add the hot liquid, while whisking, and bring to a boil; cook until thick and smooth. Fold in the chicken meat and set aside to cool.

2. For breading the croquettes: Shape the croquette batter into 14 (3-ounce) elongated cone-shaped portions, and stand them on a wax-paper-lined rimmed sheet pan or tray.

3. Whisk the eggs, milk, and salt together in a shallow bowl. Put the flour in another bowl, and the bread crumbs in a third. Dip the croquettes in the egg mixture, then into the flour, turning to coat evenly. Set aside for a couple of minutes. Finish breading the croquettes by dipping them back into the egg mixture and then rolling them in the bread crumbs. Set aside on the lined sheet pan.

4. For the chicken gravy: Melt the butter in a saucepan and then stir in the flour. Pour in the stock and whisk until smooth. Bring to a boil, then reduce the heat to a simmer and cook until slightly thick, 20 minutes. Add the fresh parsley and the salt and white pepper to taste.

5. To cook the croquettes: Heat about 4 inches of oil in a deep, heavy-bottomed pot until a deep-fry thermometer reads 350°F. Line a baking sheet with paper towels. Fry the croquettes, in batches, until golden brown, about 3 minutes. Drain and blot on the paper-towel-lined baking sheet.

6. Serve the croquettes on a bed of mashed potatoes, if desired, topped with the chicken gravy.

Silk City Philly

EST. 1958, RE-EST. 2007 ★ ONE ROCKIN' BAR CAR

★ TRACK IT DOWN ★

435 Spring Garden Street
Philadelphia, PA 19123
215-592-8838
www.silkcityphilly.com

There's more to Philadelphia than cheesesteaks. Come here to meet a French-trained chef who's putting a whole new spin on diner fried fare. We're talking pulled pork empanadas, spring rolls stuffed with duck confit and flavored with five-spice powder, shrimp and crab potstickers, and fried oyster salad. They even hand-cut the fries and fry them twice for *steak frites* Parisian-style. Chef Peter Dunmire says, "I love the French. I wouldn't have French fries if it weren't for the French."

After finishing cooking school in Paris, Peter found his career at the fifty-year-old Silk City Philly, which has been totally revamped by plumber turned restaurateur Mark Bee. He used to do the plumbing here, and when the neighborhood favorite came up for sale he couldn't resist. He renovated it his way, complete with copious red and blue neon and a velvet Elvis, and let Peter do his thing with the menu.

And Peter doesn't just do fried food well. He does supreme meatloaf with wild mushroom gravy and grilled cheese with Vermont Cheddar on thick-cut country white; and his wings are something special too: dry-rubbed with cumin, garlic, paprika, and more, then baked for forty-five minutes and fried up

Inside is one sweet velvet Elvis.

quickly before being tossed in a mixture of chipotle, butter, cayenne, hot sauce, and Dijon mustard. It's a primo wing; I'd eat these every day.

It's all about great food and good prices, and as Mark says, "We love making people happy and just throwing a party." And he's not kidding: those black velvet paintings are illuminated by disco balls in the attached club. It's one rocking bar car.

You can come out of the bottle the easy way . . . *or the hard way.*

Pork and Sweet Potato Empanadas

ADAPTED FROM A RECIPE COURTESY OF PETER DUNMIRE OF SILK CITY PHILLY

For the diner, Chef Peter uses a fresh ham and basically simmers it until it pretty much falls apart. Super tender. This dish is an orchestra—a medley of great flavor.

MAKES ABOUT 20 EMPANADAS

Pork

1 tablespoon granulated garlic

1 tablespoon coarse kosher salt

1 tablespoon smoked sweet paprika

1 tablespoon cumin powder

1 tablespoon onion powder

1 tablespoon freshly ground black pepper

1 pound boneless pork shoulder,
    cut into large cubes

Dough

2 cups all-purpose flour, plus more for sealing
    the dough

2 teaspoons baking powder

Pinch of salt

Pinch of sugar

⅓ cup vegetable shortening

⅓ cup cold water

Filling

1 cup mashed cooked sweet potato

½ cup cooked black beans

½ cup chopped fresh cilantro leaves

½ teaspoon ground cinnamon

Salt and freshly ground black pepper

Salsa

2 cups diced pineapple

¼ cup diced red onion

1 jalapeño pepper, seeded and diced

1 lime, zest finely grated, and then juiced

2 tablespoons chopped fresh cilantro leaves

Glaze

½ cup chipotle en adobo puree

½ cup honey

Oil, for frying

Fresh cilantro sprigs, for garnish

1. For the pork: Combine the spices in a large bowl. Then add the pork and toss to combine. Cover and marinate for 2 hours in the refrigerator.

2. Transfer the pork to a large pot; pour in just enough water to cover. Bring to a boil, and then adjust the heat so the liquid simmers gently. Continue to cook until the meat pulls apart easily, about 1 hour and 40 minutes. Set aside to cool. Transfer the pork to a bowl, using a slotted spoon, and then shred the pork with a fork. Add some of the cooking liquid to keep the meat moist.

3. For the dough: Whisk the 2 cups of flour, the baking powder, salt, and sugar in a large bowl. Use the pastry blender to mix in the shortening. Gradually add the cold water to make a tight dough. Knead the dough until smooth, then wrap in plastic wrap and refrigerate for 1 hour.

4. Roll the dough on a lightly floured surface into a disk about ⅛ inch thick. Cut 4-inch disks, transfer to a baking sheet, cover, and refrigerate for 30 minutes. (Excess scraps can be reformed and rerolled, if you let them rest before rolling.)

5. For the filling: Mix all the filling ingredients together and season with salt and pepper. Mix equal parts cold water and flour in a small bowl to make a loose paste for sealing the empanadas. Fill the dough disks with a generous tablespoon of the filling, brush the outer edges with the flour paste, and then fold over so they look a little like half-moon raviolis. Crimp the edges with a fork and set on a rimmed sheet pan until ready to fry.

6. For the salsa and glaze: Mix all the salsa ingredients in a medium bowl. In another bowl, whisk together the chipotle en abobo and honey to make a glaze.

7. Heat about 3 inches of oil in a deep, heavy-bottomed pot until a deep-fry thermometer reads 350°F. Line a plate with paper towels. Fry the empanadas in batches until they are golden brown, about 3 to 5 minutes. Drain on the paper towels.

8. Brush the empanadas with the chipotle-honey glaze. Place the empanadas on a bed of the salsa. Garnish with the fresh cilantro sprigs and more glaze, if desired. Serve.

Evelyn's Drive-In

EST. 1969 ★ FROM BIG-BELLY CLAMS TO LOBSTER CHOW MEIN

So here on Nanaquaket Pond they serve fresh local seafood, fried or grilled, and some great local favorites like clam cakes and fresh whole, big-neck, big-belly fried clams. Jane and Domenic Bitto stumbled upon this place twenty-two years ago. Domenic actually got lost looking for another place to buy. He stopped for lunch and bought it from Evelyn herself. They've been doing things Evelyn's way ever since.

2335 Main Road (Route 77)
Tiverton, RI 02878
401-624-3100
www.evelynsdrivein.com

The staff is a lot happier since they stopped wearing the lobster outfits.

Son, this is Onion Rings 101 . . . learn it, live it, love it!

They use a dry batter on those famous clams, shake it off, and come up with a nice thin crust post-frying. It's all seafood, and you get a monster plate of it. But they're also famous for their chowder. It's a Rhode Island chowder, which means it's clear; no cream is added to it until it's served. As one regular describes, it tastes a lot like the creamy kind, but lighter. The clams are tender and the taste is delicate (and I've never said that about chowder before). Another addictive local favorite, the fried clam cake, is great dipped in the chowder while you eat.

Yet another tradition is the lobster chow mein. The Bittos thought it was a joke when they bought the place. But it was Evelyn's recipe, and it's homemade every day. They take fresh vegetables and chicken broth and stir in Hoo-Mee chow mein gravy mix—her special ingredient (available online at www.famousfoods.com). I have seen it all. I'm in Rhode Island, I'm on the water, we're making clam things, and then they break this thing out on me. Served over chow mein noodles, it's funky but good. It's the end of the spectrum, baby. Your mind, your body, and your mouth are going, "What are you having?" But as wrong as it is, it's right.

My wife's from North Providence, so you can bet next time we go back to visit I'll be at this place again.

Rhode Island Clam Chowder

ADAPTED FROM A RECIPE COURTESY OF DOMENIC BITTO OF EVELYN'S DRIVE-IN

This is Evelyn's original recipe.

8 LARGE SERVINGS

1 gallon cold water

2 cups freshly chopped raw clams

1 medium onion, chopped

1 cup (2 sticks) unsalted butter

4 bay leaves

3 tablespoons clam base, such as Better Than Bouillon (find it at superiortouch.com)

1½ tablespoons kosher salt

½ tablespoon freshly ground black pepper

4 cups ½-inch-diced Red Bliss potatoes

Sour cream, for serving

1. Put all the ingredients except the potatoes in a large soup pot. Bring to a boil over medium-high heat. Add the potatoes and cook until tender, about 10 minutes.

2. Ladle the soup into bowls and serve with a dollop of sour cream on top.

"One of these things is not like the others . . ." Sing along, you know da words.

Panini Pete's

EST. 2006 ★ HOME OF THE STATE BIRD OF FLAVORTOWN

★ TRACK IT DOWN ★

**42½ South Section Street
Fairhope, AL 36532
251-929-0122
www.paninipetes.com**

When you think fast food, you think American, right? But really there's fast food all over the world, and here in Fairhope there's a guy who's decided to do his with a European twist. You've got to meet Panini Pete, Chef Pete Blohme. He's a classically trained chef who's cracking out those pressed Italian-style sandwiches called panini.

He cooks his own turkey with his own seasonings, he's got fresh-cut fries, fresh-cut chips, and homemade aioli, he makes his own mozzarella—and it's fast enough for the fastest lunches. Picture a sandwich place where the chef gets tomatoes from a lady with a farm stand on the corner. The mozzarella is made from fresh curd sent in from Wisconsin; stack it with basil, tomato, and balsamic vinaigrette and you've got Italian caprese panini that's help-me good. And then there's the turkey and mozzarella on focaccia. The boned turkey breast is triple-wrapped in foil with seasonings and the whole package is placed in the fryer for quick cooking time and the most tender turkey you've ever tried. It's the state bird of Flavortown, dude. Pete gave up the recipe below, aren't you lucky.

All the sandwiches get extra effort, like the herb-rubbed and seared tuna or the roast beef that's also herb-rubbed and cooked for two hours; and his dogs are rolled in homemade crepes before hitting the panini press.

And for breakfast, it's the New Orleans classic, beignets, done Panini Pete's way. They're made from fresh egg and butter dough that he scoops and fries for eight minutes until brown and puffy, then sprinkles with confectioners' sugar and lemon. Served hot. Killer.

GUY ASIDE

I gotta tell you something, the first time I made fresh mozzarella was here, with a six-foot-six dude in full kitchen gear in a tiny little panini house in Fairhope, Alabama. This is one of the places you've got to go.

Pete's Rubbed and Almost Fried Turkey Sandwich

ADAPTED FROM A RECIPE COURTESY OF PANINI PETE'S

Everything works together in this sandwich, nothing overpowers anything else. It's slam-a-jam-a-bama.

MAKES 4 SANDWICHES

1 tablespoon balsamic vinegar

3 tablespoons extra-virgin olive oil, plus more for brushing

Kosher salt and coarsely ground black pepper

Focaccia bread, about 10 inches square

3 tablespoons Dijon mustard

1 pound thinly sliced Pete's Rubbed and Almost Fried Turkey (recipe follows)

3 tablespoons thinly sliced roasted red pepper

2 cups mixed baby greens

8 ounces fresh mozzarella, sliced

3 tablespoons Garlic Mayonnaise (see page 65)

1. Whisk the vinegar and olive oil together in a small bowl and season with salt and pepper.

2. Slice the focaccia into 4 equal pieces; then slice each piece horizontally for sandwiches. Spread some of the Dijon mustard on the cut side of the bottom half of each focaccia. Top the bread evenly with turkey and peppers, and season with salt and pepper. Add baby greens, and drizzle the balsamic dressing on top. Lay the mozzarella on the greens and finish with a smear of garlic mayonnaise. Place the remaining focaccia on top to make 4 sandwiches. Brush the tops and bottoms of each sandwich with olive oil.

3. Heat a sandwich press. Cook the sandwiches, in batches if needed, until the cheese melts and the bread toasts. Serve.

Pete's Rubbed and Almost Fried Turkey

MAKES ENOUGH FOR 12 SANDWICHES

¼ cup roughly chopped garlic

¼ cup roughly chopped fresh rosemary leaves

3 tablespoons roughly chopped fresh sage leaves

Finely grated zest of 2 lemons

¼ cup kosher salt

3 tablespoons freshly ground black pepper

3 pounds boneless, skinless turkey breast

Oil, for frying

Special equipment: **deep heavy-bottomed pot, for frying the turkey**

1. Process the garlic, herbs, lemon zest, salt, and pepper in a food processor fitted with the metal blade until coarsely ground. Rub the mixture generously over the turkey breast. Roll the turkey breast into a compact shape by turning the smaller end of the breast under. Wrap tightly in 3 layers of heavy-duty aluminum foil.

2. Fill a deep heavy-bottomed pot two-thirds full with oil. Heat over medium-high until a deep-fry thermometer reads 350°F. Fry the turkey breast, wrapped in the foil, for 35 minutes or 12 minutes per pound. Carefully remove the turkey from the oil and set aside, wrapped in the foil, to cool to room temperature. Refrigerate the turkey until firm enough to thinly slice, at least 2 hours or overnight.

Once you enter this door, there's no turning back.

Pete: "Do you have rubber gloves?"
Guy: "I don't own a pair, but I have a lease with an option to buy!"

Garlic Mayonnaise

MAKES ABOUT 2 CUPS

1 large egg

2 tablespoons Dijon mustard

2 tablespoons minced garlic

Juice of 2 lemons

Kosher salt and freshly ground black pepper

2 cups vegetable oil

1. Pulse the egg, mustard, garlic, and lemon juice in a food processor fitted with a metal blade. Season with salt and pepper to taste. With the machine running, add the oil in a steady stream until the mixture is pale in color and thick. Transfer the mayonnaise to a bowl, cover, and refrigerate for at least 1 hour.

Benny's Seafood

EST. 1994 ★ EAT MO*FUNG*O MOFONGO

. . . .

When I roll into an area that I am not really familiar with, I love to check out the places and the food that only the locals know about. So here I am in Miami, and I'm told I've gotta go see a guy named Benny Ojedo and try the mofongo. Mofongo?

I get there and everybody in there tells me Benny's mofongo is just like their Puerto Rican grandmas made it. It's plantains mashed up with garlic, seasonings, and fried pork rinds (chicharrón) using a baseball-bat-size club in something that looks like a giant oak log. It's a mortar and pestle gone wild. They top

★ TRACK IT DOWN ★

. . . .

**2500 SW 107th Avenue
South Miami, FL 33165
305-227-1232**

This is the Mofongo Cancan . . . and kick! and kick!

each bowlful of mofongo with pork, chicken, beef, or seafood. Benny makes it ten different ways: there's the snapper version sautéed in butter, cilantro, and white wine. The shrimp is super tender. It's bananas. I mean plantains. Plantains is good. (Get it?)

Benny also serves shredded deep-fried plantains called spiders, tostones, conch salad, and a traditional holiday favorite: a plate of rice and pigeon peas, boiled green banana dough, and roasted pork. The roasted pork is covered in a mixture of salt, oregano, garlic, annatto-flavored oil, Sazón seasoning, olive oil, and vinegar. It cooks for five hours at 350°F, and it's the real deal.

Benny was taught to make mofongo by his mom while growing up in Cabo Rojo, Puerto Rico—the same coastal town where his wife, Wanda, grew up. He ate mofongo nightly and says, "I just couldn't get enough of it." Wanda and Benny came to Miami together about twenty years ago and couldn't find a Puerto Rican restaurant they liked. So, in great dive mom-and-pop tradition, they opened their own. Now the whole family helps run the place, and a proud mom watches over, keepin' it authentic. Benny's a wizard. It's mo*fun*go and it may be one of the best things I've eaten doing *DD&D*.

Benny's Mofongo

ADAPTED FROM A RECIPE COURTESY OF BENNY'S SEAFOOD

Alone mofongo is a side dish, but for a main dish you can complement it with any cooked meats, poultry, or seafood, serving it with a cup of chicken or fish consommé to moisten the mofongo. In Puerto Rico, Benny's grandmother would bring them big bags of chicharrón from Bayamón, a city famous for its delicious pork rinds. Here in the U.S. Benny makes his own chicharrón, but you can buy them at Latin markets.

Keep your eyes on your own paper . . . however, sharing mo*fun*go is allowed.

6 large green plantains

6 small garlic cloves

¾ cup pork rind chicharrón (available at Latin markets)

½ tablespoon kosher salt, or to taste

½ cup pure olive oil, plus more for frying

I bet this bite was hot!

1. Peel the plantains and cut into 1-inch slices. Put the plantains in a bowl of water with a pinch of salt to keep them moist until ready to cook.

2. Mash the garlic, pork rinds, ¼ tablespoon of the salt, and ¼ cup of the olive oil in a mortar with a pestle. Transfer the garlic mixture to a bowl.

3. Heat about 5 inches of oil in a deep, heavy-bottomed pot (or in a deep-fryer) until a deep-fry thermometer inserted in the oil registers 300°F. Line a plate with paper towels.

4. Drain and pat dry the plantains. Fry without crowding, in batches if necessary, until the plantains are cooked but not hard, 15 to 20 minutes. It's best to check the plantains after about 15 minutes: to do so, remove a slice from the oil and cut into it—if the center is still pink, keep cooking; if it's yellow, the plantains are ready. Transfer the plantains from the oil with a slotted spoon, and drain briefly on the paper towels.

5. Mash the fried plantains with the remaining ¼ tablespoon salt and ¼ cup olive oil until just soft. Add the garlic mixture and continue mashing until the mofongo is completely blended. Serve hot.

Keegan's Seafood Grille

EST. 1985 ★ WHERE CÉSAR SERVES UP THE SEA

You'll find this joint in a strip mall beside a pristine beach west of Tampa. The motto here is: "The customer's attitude is more important than their attire," and if it swims, this guy will cook it. From the everyday to the out-of-bounds, just wait until you try their specials.

The chef is César Labrador; he's a well-traveled Spaniard who started out as an apprentice chef on Caribbean cruise ships—which is totally grueling, by the way—and continued on to cook at restaurants all over the States. He's a serious chef with a lot of heart and soul who brings his worldly ways to his food. For

> ★ TRACK IT DOWN ★
>
> **1519 Gulf Boulevard**
> **Indian Rocks Beach, FL 33785**
> **727-596-2477**
> **www.keegansseafood.com**

GUY MEETS OCTOPUS

Then there's the octopus . . . a traditional Spanish dish that César's famous for. To cook it, he shocks it in boiling water first. (It looked to me like it already had been shocked. In my promo I held two up with one hand and said, "Hey, guys, you showed up just in time, I've got a couple of cold ones.") After it curls up in that quick hot-water bath, he marinates it for a day with some seasoning, then grills it up—always al dente. César served me up one and told me to eat it one leg at a time. He calls it the breakfast of champions, and he told me it tasted like chicken . . . funny. It had a lobster consistency, and it's not as chewy as I thought it would be. The flavor was great. I gotta hand it to him, I'd eat it again.

This is not gonna fit . . .

twenty-three years this has been his home port. César has four or five specials a night, and the customers know there's no need to look at the menu; they can just trust the blackboard. "That's why people come here three or four times a week to eat," explains co-owner Linda Labrador. "They can have something different every night." He'll do Mediterranean-style pan-roasted wahoo, baked tilapia stuffed with crabmeat and artichoke, or sautéed grouper cheeks florentine.

A personal best!

César says, "I tell you, grouper, in Florida, is it. That's what everybody eats." But in this place it ain't just another grouper sandwich. He was one of the first in Florida to blacken it and created his own blackening spice. It's heavy on the crab, paprika, and some kick—a lotta cayenne. And he makes a basting sauce, too; for that he uses some ketchup, a little hot sauce, and a little mango chutney. He goes all over the board on this—brushes it right on, sprinkles it with seasoning, and blackens it on the super-hot flat top. It's juicy, and it has nice heat from the blackening spice; that sandwich is money. So's his Jamaican seafood roast with a homemade jerk sauce cooked in a tinfoil packet, Parmesan-crusted mahimahi, and a mangrove snapper special with crawfish.

Chef César doesn't make it easy on himself, he even spends two days on a real-deal Louisiana gumbo that takes the bus to Flavortown. Check out the killer recipe that follows.

Earthquake! In Florida?

Gumbo

ADAPTED FROM A RECIPE COURTESY OF CÉSAR LABRADOR OF KEEGAN'S SEAFOOD GRILLE

This gumbo is made with thirty ingredients and trust me, every one's worth it. It has rich, deep flavor, and it begs you to eat it.

SERVES 10 TO 12

Stock

1 pound shrimp, heads on

1 tablespoon oil

3 medium live blue crabs

2 bay leaves

1 head of garlic, cut in half

1 medium onion

2 celery stalks

1 carrot

2 tablespoons crab boil seasoning, such as Old Bay

1 teaspoon crushed red pepper flakes

2 tablespoons kosher salt

Roux

1 cup peanut oil

4 chicken legs and thighs

1 cup all-purpose flour

Gumbo

½ cup oil

1 pound andouille or smoked sausage

2 large onions, chopped

5 to 6 celery stalks, chopped

3 to 4 carrots, peeled and chopped

1 large green bell pepper, stemmed, seeded, and chopped

1 tablespoon chopped garlic

2 tablespoons paprika

1 tablespoon dried oregano

1 tablespoon dried thyme

1 teaspoon granulated onion

1 teaspoon granulated garlic

1 teaspoon crushed red pepper flakes

1 teaspoon freshly ground black pepper

1 (6-ounce) can tomato paste

1 (14-ounce) can diced or stewed tomatoes

Kosher salt and freshly ground black pepper

1 pound cut okra, frozen

1 tablespoon oil

1. For the stock: Peel and head the shrimp, and set the shrimp aside. Heat the oil in a large pot, add the shrimp peels and heads, and cook until slightly toasted. Carefully add the crabs, and cover the pot to steam the crabs for 5 minutes. Add the rest of the stock ingredients, and cook until the vegetables soften, about 10 minutes. Add 2 quarts water, bring to a boil, and cook for 30 minutes. Add 2 more quarts water, return to a boil, and then simmer for 1½ hours. Strain the stock, and discard solids.

2. For the roux: Meanwhile, preheat the oven to 375°F. Heat the peanut oil in an ovenproof skillet over medium-high heat. Add the chicken and cook until brown on both sides. Transfer to a baking dish (reserve the oil in the skillet) and roast until cooked through, about 20 minutes. Set the chicken aside to cool.

3. Whisk the flour into the reserved oil and pan drippings, and cook until it begins to get lighter in color, about 2 minutes. Transfer the skillet to the oven and cook, stirring every 20 minutes, until it turns mahogany brown, about 2 hours and 20 minutes. Cool slightly.

4. For the gumbo: Heat the oil in a large pot. Add the sausage, and cook to render some of the fat. Add the vegetables and cook over medium heat, stirring occasionally. When the onions are translucent, stir in the gumbo seasonings, cooking to release their flavorful oils. Then stir in the tomato paste.

5. Add the dark roux to the gumbo and mix well. Add the diced tomatoes and half the stock. Using a wooden spoon, scrape all the good browned bits that cling to the bottom of the pot. Bring to a boil over medium heat and add more stock, as needed. After about 30 minutes, season with salt and pepper to taste. Add the okra to the gumbo and bring to a simmer.

6. Pull the chicken meat from the bones and cut into bite-size pieces. Heat a large skillet and add the tablespoon of oil. Season the shrimp with salt and pepper and cook until just curled. Add the shrimp and chicken to the gumbo and simmer for 5 to 10 minutes. Serve immediately, or set the gumbo aside in the refrigerator covered for a couple hours (or overnight) for the flavors to really come together.

Scully's Tavern

EST. 1989 ★ THE SPORTS BAR THAT SERVES ESCARGOT

. . . .

★ TRACK IT DOWN ★

**9809 Sunset Drive
Miami, FL 33173**
305-271-7404
www.scullystavern.net

Twenty years ago, a flight attendant and a carpenter took a chance on opening a restaurant. In the great tradition of *DD&D* spots, it didn't look like much, located in a strip mall in Miami. But this couple had a plan. People would call this place a sports bar, but they'd be serving escargot.

Chris Hirsh started working in the restaurant biz at fourteen and got out at twenty-six to go into construction. Then his wife, Cass, won a lottery the state of Florida runs to hand out liquor licenses. "So I said, look, you can build bars, you're a chef," says Cass. They'd never run restaurants, but they weren't going to be standard in anything they did here anyway. They set about introducing the neighborhood crowd to Chris's kind of food, and the customers loved it. As one regular says, "What does Chris do? I don't know, but it's melt-in-your-mouth delicious."

Scully's serves mussels Provençal, blackened mahimahi, seared tuna, and chicken francese. Even the bar food is over the top. Their wings are like chicken piccata on a stick. What you don't

expect, you'll get here. Chef-owner Chris explains simply, "I do this food because I worked at a French restaurant." Okay, good enough for me. And man it's good.

The potato-chip-encrusted mahimahi sandwich is a favorite here—reminds me of when I'd pile my chips on my sandwich as a kid. And it may be some of the best batter I've ever had on fish. If anybody ever says they want a fish sandwich, this should be it.

They're walking me out after an escargot marathon.

Everything's made from scratch here, from the croutons and peppercorn dressing to scampi butter with garlic, shallots, white wine, and lemon juice (which they use on their mussels Provençal); their oysters with jalapeños, lemon juice, and a little provolone; and their escargot, which are not your normal chewy snails (they're delicate, like buttah).

Now to me, Buffalo wings are hot sauce and butter and that's it. Scully's wings have a different spin, but I was willing to watch. They take a gallon of hot sauce, a half gallon of Worcestershire, fresh chopped garlic, and butter, fry the wings partly, and toss them in the sauce. Then they grill them, then they toss them, then they grill them, and . . . then you eat them. People love them. And I might get kicked out of the wing-eating club for eating his scampi wings, but the caramelized garlic is the kicker. It's some legit food.

So stop in at Scully's. A lot of people might look at the outside and pass them by, but they don't know what they're missing. You've got pool up front and guys in the back in chef's coats.

"In"crusted Dolphin (Mahimahi) Sandwich

ADAPTED FROM A RECIPE COURTESY OF SCULLY'S TAVERN

How did Chris come up with this? Well, as he says, he noticed no one wants the crushed bits at the end of a bag of potato chips, and one day he just had to do something with them. Voilà.

MAKES 6 SANDWICHES

Batter

8 large eggs

¾ cups finely grated Parmesan cheese

¼ teaspoon kosher salt

¼ teaspoon ground white pepper

1 cup fresh flat-leaf parsley leaves, chopped

Fish

Oil, for frying

6 (6-ounce) pieces dolphin (mahimahi) fillet

Flour, for dusting the fish

6 cups crushed potato chips

Assembly

6 kaiser rolls

6 thin slices onion

6 slices tomato

6 leaves green lettuce

½ cup tartar sauce

6 lemon wedges

1. For the batter: Whisk the ingredients together in a large bowl.

2. For the fish: Heat a deep-fryer, or about 4 inches of oil in a deep, heavy-bottomed pot, until a deep-fry thermometer reads 375°F. Line a plate with paper towels.

3. If the fillets are thick, butterfly them so they will cook all the way through without the potato-chip crust getting too dark. Put flour on a dish. Put the crushed potato chips in another dish.

4. Dredge the fish, one fillet at a time, in the flour and then dip into the batter, letting the excess batter drip back into the bowl. Then lay the fish in the chips, pressing and turning to coat evenly. Carefully slip the fish into the oil and fry until it floats to the surface of the oil, is golden brown, and is just cooked through, 3 to 4 minutes. Transfer the cooked fish to the paper towels to drain. Repeat with the other fillets.

5. To assemble the sandwiches: Place the fish in the rolls, and top with the onion, tomato, lettuce, and tartar sauce. Serve with the lemon wedges.

Watch, Guy, they're gonna jump right out of the fryer. (Chico the cameraman doesn't believe it.)

Ted Peters

EST. 1951 ★ A SMOKIN' TAMPA-AREA LANDMARK

★ TRACK IT DOWN ★

**1350 Pasadena Avenue
South Pasadena, FL 33707
727-381-7931**

So, I'm cruising the beach area in St. Petersburg, right outside Tampa, and I'm there because so many of you e-mailed me about this joint I have to check out: Ted Peters Famous Smoked Fish. Nice call Laura Black, George Davis, and so many more who are fifth-generation-strong regulars.

This place has been family-run for fifty-seven years. Co-owner Michael Lathrop's uncle was the guy with the name on the sign and the good idea to turn a backyard hobby smokin' fish into a business. Michael says, "Ted Peters took it from the backyard, stuck it out in the front yard, and kinda waved the traffic down as it would go by. People would put the brakes on, back up, and say, 'What's that about?'"

Today folks are still jammin' on the brakes for smoked salmon, mahimahi, and the hometown favorite, mullet, still made the same way by the same family. Walk through the John Wayne doors on the side and shake hands with Ben, a fifth-generation family smoker. Now that's a piece of history; I felt like I'd shaken the Liberty Bell. They sprinkle salt over all of the fish, then lightly brush on their secret tomato-oil–based mixture. Next it's over to the smokehouse, where Ben slots in the massive tray. You need an eagle-span reach for this job—little guys don't do it well, Michael says. They smoke with red oak and check on them every fifteen minutes, adding raw fish on the bottom and shifting up as they cook and add more. Then it's to the cooling cabinet, and then the fish is ready to be served. That's tasty.

Their chopped-up smoked fish spread is a huge seller. The spread contains mahimahi and mullet, but cook Jim

GUY ASIDE

Now, I'm not a big fan of tuna salad; to me it's a bunch of fish mixed with mayonnaise. But the smoked fish spread at Ted Peters is fantastic. And talk about history. This place used to be out here by itself, and stuff has been built up around it. It's like stepping back in time—a real Tampa-area landmark.

Hood says the mullet is the "kicker" (no fair, that's my word). What pulls it all together for me is the onion, the celery, and the smoke. A lot of locals order the Ted Peters surf and turf, which is smoked fish spread and a hamburger. And they'll tell you, they use Velveeta on their cheeseburgers, loved by regulars because it always stays melted and extra gooey. They also recommend the warm potato salad, which has hot fried bacon pieces, hot grease and all, mixed in. It's up there with some rockin' potato salads I've had, and it fits right in with the surf and turf and smoked mullet.

Bottom line, the owners know that Ted Peters is the last spot left in this area that anchors the childhood memories of the longtime locals around here. The locals are in good hands and eatin' great smoked mullet.

En vogue runway shot.

Smoked-Fish Spread

ADAPTED FROM A RECIPE COURTESY OF TED PETERS

Make sure you do all the mixing of the fish for this recipe by hand; the idea is to make it as fluffy as can be before adding the sauce.

MAKES ABOUT 3 CUPS

12 ounces boneless, skinless smoked trout

½ cup sweet relish

½ cup mayonnaise

¼ cup minced onion

¼ cup minced celery

Kosher salt and freshly ground black pepper

Crackers and Crystal hot sauce

1. Flake the fish into pieces. Then mix all the ingredients for the sauce together in a medium bowl. Gently mix the fish into the sauce and combine well to make an even spread. Season with salt and pepper to taste. Transfer to a serving dish or ramekin and fluff fish with a fork.

2. Serve the spread with crackers and Crystal hot sauce.

Marietta Diner

EST. 1995 ★ THE GREEK DINER THAT CONQUERED GEORGIA

★ TRACK IT DOWN ★

**306 Cobb Parkway North
Marietta, GA 30062
770-423-9390
www.mariettadiner.net**

Here's a classic one for you, a big, shiny steel diner run by a big extended family with a huge menu serving all kinds of food, especially Greek. You'd expect this kind of place in New Jersey or Philly, but welcome to Marietta, Georgia.

Gus Tselios grew up in a big diner family near New York City and came to Georgia with his mom, dad, cousins, and head chef Gus Garidas, "Uncle Gus," to bring the diner south. He was just out of high school, and he had noticed that the city needed a diner that would serve breakfast, lunch, and dinner twenty-four hours a day. And did it ever: the Marietta currently serves 2,500 to 3,000 people daily.

They serve gyros, souvlaki, stuffed grape leaves, baklava, and these big squares of Greek spinach pie that are handed out like dinner rolls, for free; it's a Greek touch. They make thirty to forty trays a day of the stuff, called spanakopita. It's packed with spinach and feta cheese between layers of filo dough: you can grab it like a pizza, but I give it the "cheesesteak hunch." Bend over the table, grab it around, get the interweave of the fingers going. It's awesome, so full of flavor.

Then you have to try the pasticcio—the Greek version of lasagna. It's Uncle Gus's recipe, and if you get in the way while he's making it, you might lose an arm. He's a machine. He's Picasso. Everything from the cream sauce to the meat sauce is scratch. It has a fantastic, deep, rich flavor with a shot of nutmeg and al dente pasta.

> We had a couple come from North Carolina (three hours away) just to have lunch on their day off and they said it was worth the trip. The customers who come from within fifty miles actually feel like locals now.
>
> —GUS TSELIOS, MARIETTA DINER

A couple thousand meals a day, and they plate every one up like it's going to the president. Uncle Gus serves the paella on saffron rice with lobster, scallops, mussels, even a shot of cognac in the sauce. I didn't know whether to eat it or take my picture with it. Whether you're ordering the beef stroganoff, the fettuccine alfredo, the best matzoh ball soup south of Brooklyn, or the stuffed grape leaves off the 400-plus-item menu, you're not going to leave hungry at this place.

Welcome to the Marietta Adopt-a-Cake Center!

Spinach Pie (Spanakopita)

ADAPTED FROM A RECIPE COURTESY OF GUS TSELIOS AND GUS GARIDAS OF MARIETTA DINER

TIP: Be sure to remember to sprinkle the water on the pie just before putting it in the oven. If you don't, the layers will separate under that first shot of heat and overcook.

SERVES 8

2 to 3 tablespoons olive oil

1 yellow onion, diced

3 small bunches of scallions (white and green parts), chopped

½ cup chopped fresh dill

½ teaspoon ground nutmeg

½ teaspoon freshly ground black pepper

¼ teaspoon kosher salt, or to taste if the feta is salty

3 pounds spinach, rinsed and chopped

2 pounds feta cheese, crumbled

3 large eggs

1 pound 18 by 13-inch phyllo dough sheets

1 pound unsalted butter, melted

1. Heat the olive oil in a large pot over medium high heat. Add the onion and cook until brown, stirring occasionally, about 8 minutes. Add the scallions, dill, nutmeg, black pepper, and salt, and cook, stirring occasionally, until the scallions are tender, about 4 minutes. Transfer the vegetables to a large bowl, scraping any browned bits from the pan.

2. Bring a big pot of salted water to a boil. Add the spinach and cook, stirring occasionally, until tender but still bright green. Drain in a colander and cool under cold running water. Squeeze the spinach dry by hand, to remove as much moisture as possible. Mix the spinach with the vegetables and cool.

3. Add the crumbled feta cheese and the eggs to the vegetables and mix thoroughly.

4. Preheat the oven to 350°F.

5. Lay the phyllo sheets in a stack on a cutting board. Cut in half to make two even stacks of 9 by 13-inch phyllo sheets. Cover one stack with a barely moist kitchen towel so they don't dry out.

6. Brush a 9 by 13-inch baking pan with some of the butter. Lay a sheet of phyllo in the pan and brush with butter. Continue layering half of the remaining phyllo sheets, brushing each sheet with melted butter as you layer them in the pan. Evenly spread the spinach mixture on top. Then layer and butter the remaining phyllo sheets over the filling. Cut into the top layer(s) of phyllo to mark square serving portions. Tuck the ends of dough into the pan. Sprinkle the pie lightly with a little water (as if you're blessing it).

7. Bake the pie until golden brown, about 1 hour. Serve warm or at room temperature.

They have their own nuclear power plant in the basement to light this joint up.

Rivershack Tavern

EST. 100 YEARS AGO (GIVE OR TAKE) , RE-EST. 1991 ★ FINE FOOD AND FUNK PERSONIFIED

★ TRACK IT DOWN ★

**3449 River Road
Jefferson, LA 70121
504-834-4938
www.therivershacktavern.com**

When you're cruisin' down River Road in Jefferson, Louisiana, don't expect to run into much. There's a lot of swampland, the Mississippi's right beside you, and then you find this place—and boy are you in for a surprise. It's a roadside bar with a serious restaurant kick.

The building itself is about one hundred years old, and it's been everything from a restaurant to a bar, a grocery, a liquor store, and a pharmacy. The "Shack" is funk personified. Original, brightly colored 1940s ads were uncovered on the front facade half a century after they had been hand painted, and this is the "home of the tacky ashtray," where you can get a free drink for bringing one in. When current owner Donny Thomas bought the place a few years ago, it came with a funky decor, including bright-colored bar stools that have the legs of a biker, a shrimper, a golfer, or a pirate. It also came with a loyal crowd and a classically trained chef, Mike Baskind, who does all the basics from burgers to po'boys, but knocks 'em dead with his specials.

Donny says the phone starts ringing about 8 o'clock in the morning with folks wondering what the special is, and it's whatever Mike feels like doing that day. He does a braised lamb shank with garlic, red wine, and bay leaves; "rascally rabbit" with green onion and Creole mustard spaetzle; seared ahi; alligator sausage; or snappin' turtle soup, to name a few.

Did I say turtle soup? Mike has a nicely liberal hand with bacon grease, which he uses to fry up the

It's turtle time.

It just says _party_...

holy trinity (New Orleans–style that's celery, green pepper, and onion) and adds in turtle meat, ground beef, bay leaves, diced tomatoes, grated lemon zest and juice, hard-boiled eggs, chopped spinach, sherry, and a dark roux. I'll be honest, at that point it looks like the taco salad beat up the Cobb salad and the turtle got in the middle. But it's simmered for about three hours, and everything gets along nicely after that. With a sprinkle of sherry and chopped green onions, I went Aquaman and had turtle soup. It's like a really nice stew, the texture is fantastic, the broth is really good. It's a new entry in my list of unusual delights (alongside gizzards and octopus).

Mike has yet another take on the New Orleans favorite red beans and rice. That's Monday's special. It's bacon fat, kidney beans, ham hock (holy hock, it was a big one), Worcestershire, hot sauce, the trinity, and bay leaves, and it all simmers together for four hours. It gets nice and creamy, the hock breaks down nicely, and they serve it up alongside grilled chicken or sausage with a scoop of white rice. It's too good to be good for you, and it's got a depth far beyond just regular red beans and rice. It's got that velvety I-want-more going on with it. It's just dynamite.

Spicy Southern Greens with Tasso and Andouille

ADAPTED FROM A RECIPE COURTESY OF MIKE BASKIND OF RIVERSHACK TAVERN

Just like everything Mike cooks up, this has somethin' special going on with it. All I can say is enjoy.

6 TO 8 SERVINGS

2 really large bunches of collard and turnip or mustard greens, stemmed and roughly chopped (about 10 quarts)

½ cup rendered bacon fat

8 ounces spicy Cajun tasso, diced (Tasso is a hot-smoked pork preparation common in Cajun cooking; it's made of shoulder meat with a spice blend of garlic, cayenne, and paprika.)

8 ounces andouille sausage or spicy smoked sausage, cut into thin rounds

1 cup diced onions

½ cup diced celery

½ cup diced green bell pepper

2 tablespoons chopped garlic

2 tablespoons hot sauce

1 tablespoon Worcestershire sauce

2 tablespoons cider vinegar

2 tablespoons molasses

Kosher salt and freshly ground black pepper

1. Soak the greens in a large amount of cold water; lift the greens out of the water and strain. (Do *not* pour the greens and their water over the strainer; this will simply deposit the sand and earth you are trying to remove right back on top of them.) Repeat the process until there is no more grit in the washing water. Dry the greens well.

2. Heat the bacon fat in a large heavy-bottomed pot over medium heat, add the tasso and andouille, and cook until browned, 5 to 7 minutes. Then add the onions, celery, green pepper, and garlic

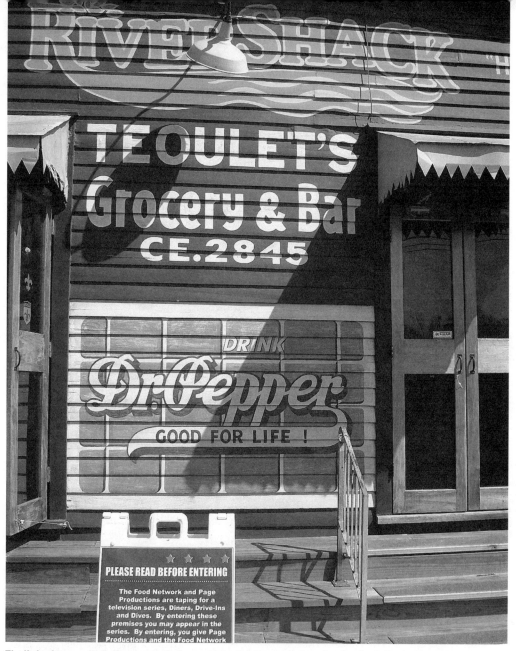

The little sign says it all: Please read before entering 'cause you might end up in a book. Yeah, this one!

and cook until the onions are translucent, about 8 minutes. Add the greens, the hot sauce, Worcestershire, vinegar, and molasses, and simmer, partially covered, until the vegetables are tender, 15 to 40 minutes depending on the mix of the greens. Season with salt and pepper to taste. Serve.

Penguin Drive-In

EST. 1954 , RE-EST. 2000 ★ FROM FRIED PICKLES TO WINKY-DINKY DOGS

★ TRACK IT DOWN ★

**1921 Commonwealth Avenue
Charlotte, NC 28205
704-375-6959
www.penguindrivein.com**

If you really want to find out if someone's from Charlotte, North Carolina, ask them where the Penguin is. If they send you to the zoo, then you know they ain't from here. Because the Penguin I'm talking about has been rockin' it for more than fifty years and makes some of the meanest pickles you'll ever try. That's right: at this Charlotte landmark, a tattooed chef is keeping families happy with a fried-pickle blue-plate special.

"Every day probably ninety percent of the tables have fried pickles on them," says chef Greg Auten. He started out working at his dad's concession stand at the fair, and since then he's worked at plenty of fine-dining restaurants and come up with plenty of recipes; but the fried pickles may be the best. Greg thinks his recipe is so popular because he keeps it pretty simple: he takes $3/16$-inch crinkle-cut hamburger dill pickles, drained of brine, and soaks them in buttermilk. Then he combines 1 pound of flour with 1 tablespoon of granulated garlic and 1 teaspoon of cayenne pepper. He tosses the pickles in the mixture, shakes off the excess flour, and fries them in oil at 350°F for 3 to 4 minutes, until golden brown. Served up with some cold ranch dressing and enjoyed with the chef-recommended cold beverage or beer, and you're good to go. How do they taste? Wow. Even people who don't like pickles can't get enough of these.

When this place opens its doors on a Sunday morning, it's kind of like bumper cars. You know: you're in line and when you finally get to the front you run to the car you want. It's immediately packed. Folks say they're will-

GUY ASIDE

I just revisited the Penguin, a year after the show was shot. Apparently, the guys were out celebrating the night after we wrapped, they were enjoying the success of it, and one of them broke his leg. I guess they always said, you know, break a leg! My wife said the deep-fried pickles were the best she ever had.

I'll take that car . . . and that one . . . and that one . . . and that one . . .

HISTORY OF THE PENGUIN

The Penguin was originally an ice cream parlor, a superior icon of American family life. Then in 1954 it became the Penguin Drive-In, filled with more teenagers and young singles than toddlers, but it was still a family landmark and was affectionately called "The Bird" by locals. The '70s and '80s were more difficult for the troubled Charlotte neighborhood where the Penguin resides, and the place became a bit seedy, but revitalization came about in the '90s, making the area one of Charlotte's most popular places to live. Then Jimmy King and Brian Rowe came around, wanting to open up a bar. They bought the place, but the zoning said they had to serve food. So, Brian called up Greg Auten that night and asked him to join the team as chef. After all, Greg had catered his wedding, and what better omen for success? A partnership was born and a major renovation ensued on this erstwhile burger joint. What a story about three buddies who get together and make it happen. One does construction, one does operations, and the other does the chefing. The rest is fried-pickle history.

ing to line up here because it's more than fast food. It's the real deal. Chef Greg believes the more homemade stuff they can make, the better. Like the southern flavors few people make from scratch anymore—homemade pimento cheese and corn dogs. They've got all kinds of great stuff here: outta-bounds, flattened-on-the-flip burgers that stack three patties high, a "winky-dinky dog" with chili and pimento cheese, a grilled banana and peanut butter sandwich, even black-bean hummus. It's an eclectic mix on the menu and in the crowd, and it's a family place that still kinda looks like a biker bar. Chef Greg has a tattoo referencing an old Kiss song, "King of the Night Time World," and he jokes, "I'm kinda king of the late afternoon now."

Greg's father passed away two days before the show aired, but I know he would have been so proud of Greg's achievements.

> You guys have turned the whole world on to fried pickles. I guess I've achieved sort of a cult following, and I couldn't be happier. Thank you!
>
> —GREG AUTEN,
> PENGUIN DRIVE-IN

Black Bean Hummus

ADAPTED FROM A RECIPE COURTESY OF GREG AUTEN, CO-OWNER OF PENGUIN DRIVE-IN

NOTE FROM THE CHEF: "I've always been the kind of person to ask, 'Why not?' When people say two things can't go together, I at least have to try! Traditional hummus is great, but I wondered what would happen if you added black beans, lime juice, cinnamon, and chili powder. Well, now we know: it's one of our best-sellers, and other restaurants have followed suit. I guess I'm an innovator in Middle Eastern–Mexican fusion cuisine."

MAKES ABOUT 2¾ CUPS

1 (15.5-ounce) can garbanzo beans, rinsed and drained

1 (15.5-ounce) can black beans, rinsed and drained

⅔ cup blended oil (equal parts olive and canola oil)

⅓ cup water

1 tablespoon tahini

2 small garlic cloves, chopped

4 teaspoons chili powder

Juice of 1½ limes, or to taste

1¼ teaspoons kosher salt, plus more to taste

1 teaspoon cayenne pepper

Pinch of ground coriander

Pinch of ground cinnamon

Pinch of ground cumin

Pita chips, for serving

1. Mix all the ingredients for the hummus in a bowl. Puree the hummus mixture, in batches if needed, in a food processor until very smooth. Taste and season with salt. Transfer the hummus to a serving bowl.

2. Serve with pita chips.

The Penguin Pimento Cheese

ADAPTED FROM A RECIPE COURTESY OF GREG AUTEN

NOTE FROM THE CHEF: "Pimento cheese was a kind of no-brainer for me in creating this menu because my mother either made it or bought it premade. It was one of those things that we seemed to always have, so I tweaked a recipe and now we sell fifteen to twenty pounds per day. That's a lot of winky-dinky dogs, which is certainly something we're known for!"

MAKES ABOUT 2 QUARTS

1 pound coarsely grated Cheddar cheese

½ pound coarsely grated pepper Jack cheese

⅔ cup mayonnaise

1 (4-ounce) can diced pimentos, not drained

1½ teaspoons green pepper sauce

Heaping ¼ teaspoon granulated garlic

Heaping ¼ teaspoon granulated onion

½ teaspoon freshly ground black pepper

⅛ teaspoon cayenne pepper (or less if desired)

Saltines or your favorite crackers, for serving

Now, that's a party penguin.

1. Mix all the ingredients for the spread together in a medium bowl (note that it's easier if the cheese is cold). Transfer into ramekins or other small serving dishes. Cover and refrigerate until set, at least 30 minutes.

2. Serve with crackers.

Harold's Restaurant

EST. 1932 ★ WORLD-FAMOUS MEATBALL MAGIC AND FATBACK

....

★ TRACK IT DOWN ★

602 N. Limestone Street
Gaffney, SC 29340
864-489-9153
www.haroldsrestaurant.com

In Gaffney, South Carolina, thirty minutes north of Greenville, football is king, Main Street is alive and well, and there's a little place called Harold's where you can get a chili burger for a buck and a quarter. That's my kind of joint.

The burger is more than messy, and I've never seen anything like it. There's no formal hamburger patty, and it sits in its own sauce. I told the owner, Tony Lipscomb, they'd call that a meatball in New York City. He rolls out ten to twelve thousand of these a week, and he's so proud of these burgers, he says they're the reason he bought this place twelve years ago. The secret recipe hasn't changed since 1932, and it was part of the deal. They're addictive. Tony once saw a guy eat fifteen of them in one sitting, and then come back for supper.

This brand of meatball magic starts with one pile of meatballs that are made to break down into the chili, and one pile that you see on the bun. So I had to ask. If they're gonna be mashed up into the sauce, why make them into meatballs in the first place? Tony's answer: "That's the way it's been done for seventy-five years, and that's the way we've continued on doing it." Now, the cooking method of the meatball that's the meat that goes into the sauce was part of the secret they couldn't show me. So I went and stood in the corner. He then mashed up the browned meatballs and put them into the pot along with the whole meatballs that had been cooked (while I stood in the corner). The next step was making the "soup," with a little chili powder, a little paprika, a little garlic powder, onion powder, salt, and pepper cooked up in tomato sauce. They combine that with the meatballs and take it out front. An original all-the-way is mustard, onions, and chili (with meatballs) on a bun. It reminds me a little bit of a sloppy Joe meets a hamburger meets chili, and I really have to say the killer is that steamed bun and the fresh onions.

They also throw the chili over dogs—the famous way is mustard, onion, and chili (no meatball). I'd still like to know how they make that chili, but I'd have to buy the place.

All they do here is down-home cooking. There's not a can in the place, you've got grilled homemade pimento cheese sandwiches, rich chicken stew, fresh corn muffins, and something called fatback. The Wednesday special is pinto beans and fatback. Fatback? It's a strip of fat taken from a hog's back. They slice it ¼ inch thick. The meat (the pork fat) is attached to the rind and it's salt cured, much like bacon. Then the fatback is thrown in the oven on a greased baking sheet to cook for 45 minutes at 400°F until lightly brown and crispy. Tony makes pinto beans with shredded ham and serves it up with corn bread and the fatback with homemade chowchow relish. His method of eating this medley: Throw some corn bread, a couple pieces of onion, and some chowchow into your pinto beans and take a bite. Then take a bite of fatback to finish it off. I gotta tell you, with the chowchow in there, that's off the hook.

Looks on with amazement and says, "He actually believed me. Fatback and chow chow at the same time! Sucker!"

World-Famous Chowchow

ADAPTED FROM A RECIPE COURTESY OF HAROLD'S RESTAURANT

We couldn't get the chili recipe, but this chowchow recipe's a classic.

MAKES 6 CUPS

1⅓ cups vinegar

1 cup sugar

6 small green bell peppers, stemmed, seeded, and diced

6 medium green tomatoes, diced

1 small red bell pepper, stemmed, seeded, and diced

1 small yellow onion, diced

2 cups roughly chopped green cabbage

2 jalapeño peppers, stemmed

2 teaspoons kosher salt

1. Combine the vinegar and sugar in a medium nonreactive pot and bring to a simmer. Pulse each vegetable individually until coarsely ground in a food processor fitted with a metal blade. Add the vegetables to the vinegar and simmer for 5 minutes. Add the salt.

2. Can according to standard USDA instructions, or see www.homecanning.com

This picture will make my mom, Penny, proud: me with a mouth full of food!

Pizza Palace

EST. 1961 ★ BRINGING RED SAUCE TO ROADSTERS

★ TRACK IT DOWN ★

**3132 E. Magnolia Avenue
Knoxville, TN 37914
865-524-4388
www.visitpizzapalace.com**

So I'm cruisin' through Knoxville, Tennessee, and I'm thinking to myself, Self, I'm feeling like some pasta and maybe some pizza. So when I see the Pizza Palace up ahead I know I'm in. I mean, Italian food at a drive-in? I've got to check this place out. This Knoxville establishment brings slam-a-jam pizza and red sauce to roadsters. I mean they are turnin' and burnin.' Totally authentic, made-from-scratch Italian food at this place that's been a go-to spot in this town for nearly half a century.

Sam Peroulas and his cousin Charlie are running the Pizza Palace just like their dads, Al and Arthur, did after they arrived from Greece with their brother Gus in the 1950s. The brothers stuck together, learned English, and set about learning the restaurant business, eventually opening three. "On opening day in 1961 they were lining out the door as a band played in the parking lot," says Charlie. "This was the first experience with pizza that many people in Knoxville had. It wasn't widely available in 1961." In fact, it was one of the first pizza places in East Tennessee.

> **A woman called for directions from the Knoxville airport. She wasn't going to stop anywhere, just straight to Pizza Palace. We've met at least one person from every state in the U.S. No joke.**
>
> —CHARLIE PEROULAS, PIZZA PALACE

Needless to say, the pizza befits the restaurant's name. Charlie points out, "A lot of people will advertise fresh ingredients, but frozen dough is not a fresh ingredient." Their dough is made from yeast and flour and is left to rise overnight, then kneaded, tossed, and topped with sauce and all the classic toppings.

If pizza brought to your car seems weird, wait until you hear what a lot of people order to go with it: huge, sweet stacks of the biggest-ever onion rings, fresh-sliced then dipped in milk and seasoned flour before frying. People don't come here just for pizza. The Palace is very well known for their Greek and chef salads (made to feed an army), square hamburgers, homemade desserts, and pasta served with a made-from-scratch sauce filled with meat. Don't ask for marinara on your pasta. Owner Sam Peroulas says, "There's no vegetarians in Knoxville, are you crazy? We're carnivores down here." They take a top round of USDA choice beef (for a meat sauce!), grind it up, and combine it with a ton of chopped onions that have been simmering in butter and a secret-recipe tomato base. The sauce must then simmer all day long before serving; it's aromatic torture.

Sam and Charlie are keeping it real: not a corner is cut, and they make everything fresh every day, just like their dads did. "We have a very sentimental attachment to the business," explains Charlie. "My dad worked very long and hard to give me opportunities he never had, and what better tribute than giving back to him and continuing the tradition."

A lot of the equipment in this place has been here from the beginning. This is the hard-wired, nobody-makes-'em-anymore order phone, for which they diligently track down spare parts. Just think: this same phone has been used since 1961, when they bought it.

Coconut Cream Pie

ADAPTED FROM A RECIPE COURTESY OF PIZZA PALACE

The famous family recipes at Pizza Palace don't stop at pizza and sauce, and this classic coconut cream pie is the proof in the pudding.

MAKES 1 (10-INCH) PIE

3 cups whole milk, divided

3 large eggs

½ cup plus 2 tablespoons cornstarch

¾ cup sugar

2 tablespoons unsalted butter

⅛ teaspoon fine salt

1¼ cups untoasted shredded sweetened coconut, plus ⅓ cup, toasted

1 teaspoon pure vanilla extract

1 (10-inch) prepared baked pie crust

Whipped cream (optional)

1. Whisk ½ cup of the milk, the eggs, and the cornstarch in a bowl until smooth.

2. In a medium saucepan, whisk together the rest of the milk with the sugar, butter, and salt. Bring just to a boil over medium heat. Slowly whisk in the egg mixture. Continue to cook, whisking constantly, until the mixture just comes to a boil and is very thick. Remove from the heat and whisk in the 1¼ cups of untoasted coconut and the vanilla.

3. Pour the coconut custard into the pie crust. Spread evenly into the crust and scatter the toasted coconut on top. Refrigerate until chilled and set, about 2 hours.

4. Slice and serve—with whipped cream, if desired.

Black-Bottom Pie

ADAPTED FROM A RECIPE COURTESY OF PIZZA PALACE

If you're from the south, this recipe will strike a familiar, deep custard-filled chord.

MAKES 1 (10-INCH) PIE

1 ounce semisweet chocolate, finely chopped

3 cups whole milk, divided

3 large eggs

½ cup plus 2 tablespoons cornstarch

¾ cup sugar

2 tablespoons unsalted butter

⅛ teaspoon fine salt

1 teaspoon pure vanilla extract

1 (10-inch) prepared graham cracker crust

Whipped cream (optional)

1. Put the chocolate in a medium bowl.

2. In another bowl, whisk ½ cup of the milk, the eggs, and the cornstarch until smooth.

3. In a medium saucepan, whisk together the rest of the milk with the sugar, butter, and salt. Bring just to a boil over medium heat. Slowly whisk in the egg mixture. Continue to cook, whisking constantly, until the mixture just comes to a boil and is very thick. Remove from the heat, add the vanilla, and add half the custard to the chocolate. Let stand until the chocolate melts.

4. Whisk the chocolate custard until smooth and pour into the prepared crust. Set aside until the custard is set, about 10 minutes. Then spread the remaining custard on top. Refrigerate until chilled and set, about 2 hours.

5. Slice and serve—with whipped cream, if desired.

Tom's Bar-B-Q

EST. 1978 ★ SERIOUS 'CUE WITH A MEDITERRANEAN KICK

. . . .

★ TRACK IT DOWN ★

**4087 Getwell Road
Memphis, TN 38118
901-365-6690
www.tomsbarbq.com**

On our Memphis barbecue tour, people told us we had to come check out the rib tips at this place—and the floor show, too. They do the turn and burn, they move and shake. Owner Adam Itayem's got fifteen people working in here—and in this business you've got to do volume to make it. I haven't seen musical groups that are this in sync. Let me tell you somethin', the rib tips they're doing blow your mind. This dude is the culinary conductor on the train to Flavortown.

Just watch the guy with a knife chopping the 'cue. Adam says the guy hasn't lost a finger yet as he yells, "Let it fly, baby, let it fly!" Shouting out orders: "I've got a pork chop combo with slaw, make it hot just like this lady, please. Sauce on the side, SOS." I felt like I was a stockbroker on the floor, with my buddy Cohen.

You come in here, place your order at the counter, then take the right paper bag. You get your food in about a minute. This is speed barbecue with all the classics: briskets, ribs, chopped pork, chicken, turkey, and pork chops—with, get this, a Mediterranean kick!

The original owner was from Greece, and the recipes are treated with a Greek-style rub. Like one regular said emphatically, "If it's not broke, you don't fix it." It's crazy good. Adam bought this place from a dude named, yeah, Tom, sixteen years ago. He never even knew it existed; it looked to him like an old rustic shack, but with people just hanging out the door—which meant eating here took time. Adam fixed that.

Here's Adam, your conductor of the Flavor Train.

It took hours to clear the people for this shot.

This is the Greek-style dry rub.

They serve about fifteen hundred to two thousand people a day. It's efficient and it fits the area. It's in an industrial park and most lunches are on a time card—about thirty minutes total.

Now about those rib tips. They get them specially cut. They're not from the loin, they're a St. Louis style that's shaved right from the top above the loin, on an angle. That's not easy to find. The rub—which you've got the recipe for on page 105, and which has loads of thyme, oregano, and even pickling spice—is sprinkled onto the rib tips and marinated for twenty-four hours. Then they open the pit up and throw them on for an hour and a half to two hours. The tips come out super tender. They are off the track.

The menu's got eleven main items, nine sides, and two kinds of fries. Traditional Memphis style serves the sauce on the side. They even do marinated thick-sliced, dry-rubbed bologna. That's something you haven't seen at home before, and certainly something that just popped into my world. I'll take six to go, with slaw and sauce.

BBQ Bologna Sandwich

ADAPTED FROM A RECIPE COURTESY OF TOM'S BAR-B-Q

This is a local classic, and they do it Tom's way, with the famous rub and sauce.

MAKES 6 SANDWICHES

6 (½-inch-thick) slices of beef bologna (about 1¼ pounds)

⅓ cup Tom's BBQ Rub (recipe follows)

1 cup Tom's BBQ Sauce (see page 105)

1 tablespoon oil

6 sesame seed burger buns

3 tablespoons mayonnaise

¾ cup coleslaw

1. Rub the bologna all over with the rub. Generously brush with some of the barbecue sauce. Place the bologna in a container, cover, and refrigerate overnight.

2. When ready to serve, scrape excess rub and sauce off the bologna. Heat a large skillet over medium heat. Add the oil and fry the bologna, turning once, until it is charred on both sides, 1 to 2 minutes.

3. Place the bologna in the buns. Top each slice with some mayonnaise, coleslaw, and more barbecue sauce. Serve.

Tom's BBQ Rub

MAKES ABOUT 1½ CUPS

¼ cup crushed red pepper flakes

2 tablespoons seasoned salt

2 tablespoons salt

2 tablespoons freshly ground black pepper

2 tablespoons dried oregano

2 tablespoons dried thyme

1 tablespoon chili powder

1 tablespoon paprika

1 tablespoon granulated garlic

1 tablespoon celery salt

1 tablespoon onion powder

1 tablespoon pickling spice

¼ teaspoon ground nutmeg

1. Combine all the ingredients in a container with a tight-fitting lid. Keeps for up to 6 months.

Tom's BBQ Sauce

MAKES ABOUT 4 CUPS

4 cups tomato paste

1 cup water

¼ cup light corn syrup

2 tablespoons brown sugar

1 tablespoon white vinegar

1 tablespoon Worcestershire sauce

1 tablespoon minced onion

1 tablespoon garlic powder

½ teaspoon dried mustard

1½ teaspoons natural smoke flavor

1½ teaspoons chili powder

2 tablespoons BBQ Rub (recipe above)

1. Combine all the ingredients in a medium saucepan and simmer, partially covered, stirring occasionally for 2 hours until slightly thickened.

Dot's Back Inn

EST. 1990 ★ LITTLE HOUSE ON THE BIG FLAVOR

Check out this place in Richmond and you'll discover it's kinda like a small compact car with a big super-charged engine comin' out of the hood. It's a small, nondescript joint with tons of custom-built food.

Culinary Institute of America grad Jimmy Tsamouras had been eating here for fifteen years and, promising he wouldn't

★ TRACK IT DOWN ★

4030 Macarthur Avenue
Richmond, VA 23227
804-266-3167

People were trapped inside for hours because of the Camaro!

Take the picture—my sailor sandwich is getting cold.

change it, finally convinced owner Cookie Giannini to sell the place after sixteen years of business. The old-time customers are still coming back, so Jimmy's doing something right. He excels at familiar, varied dishes with his own custom twist. He makes a chicken Macarthur that's made with sautéed garlic, onion, sliced chicken, artichoke hearts, kosher salt and white pepper, white wine, and some al dente spaghetti—all tossed with a little bit of feta and tomatoes, then scattered with a few chopped scallions and Parmesan. Mmm-mmm. I couldn't describe it immediately, I mean it's like talking in the middle of an opera. Can't you hear it singing? There's not enough feta in pasta dishes; that feta pops and gives it a nice briny, salty, vinegary type of mmm.

Jimmy's pigs in a blanket are made with andouille from Louisiana, and his corn cakes are topped with black beans, melted cheese, some sour cream, onions, peppers, tomatoes, and salsa. Even the pizza is something different: on a pita with green sauce instead of red. The Mediterranean pie is made with walnut pesto and topped with tomatoes and feta cheese. Another favorite is the sailor sandwich. It's grilled knockwurst, pastrami, Swiss, grilled rye bread, and Dijon mustard. You can't knock the wurst. He's got the balance and could compete with any New York deli.

So next time you're in Richmond, check out Dot's; Jimmy's doing it right in a little house with big flavor.

Chunky Monkey Pancakes

ADAPTED FROM A RECIPE COURTESY OF DOT'S BACK INN

This recipe's got the whole banana and it's all wrapped up.

2 SERVINGS

Your favorite pancake batter

½ cup chocolate chips

1 cup chopped walnuts

2 bananas, peeled

Ground cinnamon

2 tablespoons unsalted butter

Whipped cream, for serving

Confectioners' sugar, for serving

Hey, that's Matt (Beaver) filming his mom . . . how cool.

1. On a greased griddle or large skillet, ladle about ¼ cup batter to make a large pancake, about 9 inches in diameter. Once bubbles start to appear on the surface, sprinkle half of the chocolate chips and walnuts on top of the pancake. Flip the pancake when golden brown, and cook until set. Transfer to a plate. Repeat to make another pancake.

2. While the pancakes cook, sprinkle ½ teaspoon cinnamon or to taste over the whole bananas. Melt the butter in a small frying pan over medium heat. When the foam subsides, place the bananas in the pan and sauté, turning, until tender.

3. Wrap each banana in a chocolate chip pancake. Garnish with whipped cream and confectioners' sugar.

Guess who made who laugh first?

Virginia Diner

EST. 1929 ★ PEANUT (AND BISCUIT) CAPITAL OF THE WORLD

★ TRACK IT DOWN ★

**322 W. Main Street
Wakefield, VA 23888
888-823-4637
www.vadiner.com**

If you're heading to the beach on Route 460 in Virginia you'll see some pretty amazing things, such as where the first peanut crop was planted in America, and right down the street from there another piece of history: Virginia Diner, serving up all kinds of southern favorites since 1929.

Fried chicken, collard greens, ham biscuits, candied yams, black-eyed peas with stewed tomatoes, coleslaw . . . all made the way they've been doing it since the beginning, when the diner was a Sussex-Surry railroad dining car on the side of the road. Owner Bill Galloway bought it in 1976 and general manager Mike Stennett came on board six years ago.

Collards are the greens of choice in these parts. They start with mammoth fresh leaves grown locally—enough to fill a huge pot—chop 'em up, and add a hunk of butter, sugar, a little water, and some Virginia smoked ham skins (from a smokehouse twenty-five minutes away). That cooks on low for three hours. It's smoky, tender, and delicious. Anybody who thinks they don't like collard greens maybe just hasn't had them the right way. These melt in your mouth.

For their ham biscuits, they slice the ham thin and put it in there while the scratch-baked buttermilk biscuit is hot. That could be the only thing they had on the menu and I'd move here. A man could survive on ham biscuits alone. I tried rolling the biscuits with Bill, and his came out like King Kong biscuits and mine like petite flowers. I gotta practice, but they still came out pretty amazing. Bill and I were speaking biscuit-ese. He says he loves biscuit-ese.

You can get light and fluffy spoon bread—an old-style corn bread that's firmer than pudding—and a mac and cheese that doesn't cut any corners, with roux, Cheddar, and American all double-baked. Order an entrée and you get two veggies—and mac and cheese is considered a veggie. That's my kinda veggie.

Bill came in here to make it happen. He says pleasing people is the greatest pleasure he gets. My friend, you made it happen.

Look at that focus, like a surgeon.

Peanut Pie

ADAPTED FROM A RECIPE COURTESY OF CHRIS EPPERSON OF VIRGINIA DINER

This peanut pie is a cross between peanut cookie, peanut brittle, and pie. That's good eats.

MAKES 1 (9-INCH) PIE

8 ounces salted Virginia peanuts

3 large eggs

1 cup sugar

½ cup all-purpose flour

1⅓ cups light corn syrup

1 tablespoon unsalted butter, melted

1 blind-baked 9-inch pie crust

Whipped cream (optional)

1. Preheat the oven to 350°F.

2. Crush the peanuts with a rolling pin or mallet.

3. Lightly beat the eggs. Then whisk in the sugar and flour until well combined. Add the corn syrup and peanuts, and then the butter.

4. Pour the filling into the prepared crust. Bake for 45 to 50 minutes, or until the pie is a rich golden brown, set around the edges but still a little loose in the center. (If the crust gets dark, tent the edges with a pie shield or foil in the last part of baking.)

5. Cool to room temperature. Serve with whipped cream, if desired.

Either this is a really old picture or we need to get a new camera.

The peanut posse!

Hillbilly Hot Dogs

EST. 1999 ★ THEY GOT THE WEENIES

★ TRACK IT DOWN ★

**6591 Ohio River Road
Lesage, WV 25537
304-762-2458
www.hillbillyhotdogs.com**

So I'm rolling through my father's home state of West Viriginia and I think, this is great, it might shed some light on how he learned how to cook. What better place to start than here at Hillbilly Hot Dogs?

When Sonny Knight brought his California wife, Sharie, back home to West Virginia, this self-proclaimed hillbilly and his bride decided to open up the ultimate WV hot dog stand. "I brought Beverly Hills to the Hillbilly," says Sonny. And man, can she "yeehaw!," to the tune of a cowbell and Sonny's harmonica. Better than a native.

They've got every yard-sale item in the world in front—like that pink flamingo companion, the polka-dot-dressed lady's backside—and two schoolbuses pulled up to a shack. The buses are wall-to-wall with customers' signatures, and they serve as the indoor dining. Hillbilly's menu is stacked with every type of dog, from taco to pizza, egg dog to deep-fried, and it's up to a full pound of meat between the buns.

The chili meat sauce has been lovingly described as the closest thing one regular has found to what they served him in high school. The recipe originated from Sonny's mother. You take ground meat, mix it up with some water, and break it down into fine pieces (with plastic-gloved hands—why dirty a spoon, as Sharie says—but I wanted to opt for hip waders, that vat was so big). Then they throw in some hot pepper flakes, black pepper, salt, onion powder, garlic, chili powder, and tomato paste and heat it on the burner.

She made me a dog with jalapeños, nacho cheese sauce, barbecue sauce, mustard, mayonnaise, ketchup, then her meat sauce,

GUY ASIDE

Without a question this is one of the most insane joints I've ever been in.

onion, coleslaw, a little bit of the relish, and kraut: sounds like she was making soup. But I bit into that thing and I swear, you go through the layers and wow, it's *tasty.* That jalapeño is spicy in there, but there's a spicier version named for U.S. Congressman Nick Rahall. He created it himself and they call it Rahall's Red Hot Weenie. It's got sauerkraut, grilled onions, green peppers, jalapeños, and habanero sauce. It'll make you break a sweat, no joke.

But they're not all designed by famous people: Stacy's Flu Shot is just a weenie piled up with jalapeños. Chuck, another customer, asked for every condiment they have so they call it Chuck's Junk Yard Dog. A Home Wrecker is a fifteen-inch, one-pound all-beef weenie that's deep-fried in canola oil, then topped with jalapeños, sautéed onions and peppers, nacho cheese, chili sauce, mustard, ketchup, slaw, tomato, lettuce, and shredded cheese. Yeah, I tried that too. It was bigger than my head. And it was good.

The big bleached polar bear attacks hamburger land (movie to follow).

Rahall's Red Hot Weenie

ADAPTED FROM A RECIPE COURTESY OF SHARIE KNIGHT OF HILLBILLY HOT DOGS

MAKES 1 SERVING

1 (6-inch) all-beef hot dog, split down the middle

1 (6-inch) hot dog bun

Jalapeño-based nacho cheese sauce

Habanero Sauce (recipe follows)

Grilled jalapeños

Grilled onions

Grilled green peppers

Sauerkraut

1. Preheat a grill over medium-high heat.

2. Place the split hot dog and the bun onto the grill. Once the bun is toasted, place a border of the nacho cheese sauce around the edges of the bun. This will act as glue to keep the hot dog open, ready for stuffing. Once the hot dog is finished, place it in the bun. Spoon the habanero sauce down the middle and top with grilled jalapeños, onions, and green peppers to taste. Finish with sauerkraut to taste.

Congressman Nick Rahall and me talkin' the hot dog platform for 2012.

Me calling 3D headquarters: "This is agent Guido. Are you *sure* this is where I'm supposed to be?"

Habanero Sauce

2 large carrots, peeled and sliced

6 habanero chiles, stemmed, seeded, and quartered

2 teaspoons butter

2 teaspoons chopped garlic

2 tablespoons apple cider vinegar

Salt and freshly ground black pepper

1. Finely chop the carrots and habanero chiles in a food processor.

2. Melt the butter in a medium saucepan over medium-high heat. Add the chopped garlic, then add the carrot-habanero mixture and cook, stirring frequently, until the carrots are soft. Stir in the apple cider vinegar and season with salt and pepper to taste. Then add 1 cup water and simmer until the mixture is thick enough for spreading, about 15 minutes. Cool and serve.

Hackney's on Harms

EST. 1939 ★ HOME OF BEBE'S HACKNEYBURGERS

★ TRACK IT DOWN ★

**1241 Harms Road
Glenview, IL 60025
847-724-5577
www.hackneys.net**

It's not often that you find yourself cruising a residential area looking for a place to eat, but the locals here in Glenview say this is the spot. Right behind Grandma's house is this joint, and they say the burgers are the bomb.

There's a lot of fun in these buns and, as one regular puts it, coming here is a part of growing up in the 'burbs north of Chicago. The number-one burger is the Hackneyburger, an eight-ounce oblong patty that they've been getting from the same butcher for thirty years. But then there's the inside-out burger that's stuffed with Cheddar and bacon and the blue cheese burger that's got the cheese mixed into the meat before it's grilled. The menu's packed with home-made favorites like a brick of onion rings, a bowl of chili, and a whole range of home-baked desserts like Key lime pie.

But that burger is sublime, and it's been that way since 1939. During the Prohibition era, Bebe Hackney and her husband, Jack, started serving corned beef sandwiches from the illegal beer bar she was running from her glassed-in back porch. Once Prohibition was repealed they expanded the garage to accommodate a four-burner kitchen, wherein Bebe cooked up Hackneyburgers for the first time on ten-inch iron frying pans and served them on the dark rye bread she'd learned to make as a child for her family after her mother died.

Current owner Bill Blair says they gave the food away in the old days, like peanuts with beer. Wow, I wish that were still the program! But it really is a burger emporium. For their blue cheese burger, they take their eight-ounce patty and mix about one ounce of blue cheese into the meat. Toward the end

GUY ASIDE

I had just done the inside-out burger on my show *Guy's Big Bite* when I came here; pretty funny. This is the place where people come back to eat after they've moved away.

of grilling, more blue cheese is melted on the top. That is rich. They still serve the Hackneyburger on their fresh dark rye, and the onion ring loaf was first devised on a Friday fish fry night back in the early 1950s. They had run out of the lake perch that a customer ordered, so a cook there named Carmen said, "In the meantime I'm going to fix you something you're never going to forget." She breaded up some onion rings, fried them in a basket, and that was the birth of the "Hackney." Oh, man it's good—and worth about six trips to the gym.

Are those burger elves out front?

Another "onion" brick in the wall.

Hackney's Inside-Out Burger

ADAPTED FROM A RECIPE COURTESY OF BILL BLAIR OF HACKNEY'S ON HARMS

This is soft and cheesy on the inside, with a crunch of bacon. Mmm-mmm. Current chef Ed Hebson showed me the method with the lid of a mayonnaise jar. It works!

MAKES 4 BURGERS

2 pounds ground beef

4 ounces bacon, cooked and chopped

1 cup grated Cheddar cheese

Salt and freshly ground black pepper

2 tablespoons canola or olive oil

4 hamburger buns (optional)

Special equipment: 1 (4-inch) ring mold (a large lid of a mayonnaise jar works); plastic wrap

1. Divide the ground beef into 8 even portions. Line a round mold (or lid) with plastic wrap. Pat a portion of the meat into the mold. Top with a quarter of the bacon and cheese, taking care that the fillings aren't too close to the edge. Cover with another portion of ground beef and press the edges together to seal in the fillings. Remove the burger from the mold by the plastic wrap and shape into an even patty. Repeat to make 4 inside-out burgers.

2. Season the burgers with salt and pepper. Heat the oil in a large skillet over medium-high heat, add the burgers, and fry, turning once, until the cheese melts and the burgers are cooked to the desired degree of doneness. Serve the burgers solo or on a bun.

Smoque

EST. 2006 ★ NOT JUST ANOTHER PRETTY SAUCE

★ TRACK IT DOWN ★

**3800 N. Pulaski Road
Chicago, IL 60641
773-545-7427
www.smoquebbq.com**

On *Triple D* I'm always on the hunt for barbecue. I love to look at it, I love to make it, and I really love to eat it. So when I'm rolling through Chicago and I hear there are these dudes doing barbecue up right, I just gotta check out Smoque.

Texas brisket, Memphis-style ribs, pulled pork drenched in Carolina sauce, even baked beans the way they do them in Kansas City—it's a lineup of the best of the best. These guys got out of high tech to travel the country eating barbecue. They just decided they'd rather make ribs. Owner Barry Sorkin had never been trained as a chef, but he was and is a barbecue fanatic, and his dream was to bring it all back home to Chicago. He just hoped people would show up—and they did.

Their brisket is their best-seller, which was a huge surprise. In fact they didn't even put it on the menu originally because Chicago is traditionally a sweet-sauce-and-ribs kind of town. But the dry-rubbed brisket is selling out. For the ever-important rub he includes ground coriander, ginger, lemon pepper, ground cloves, citric acid, kosher salt, and plenty of black pepper. They smoke them overnight using a mix of apple wood and oak. Come to papa. Holy bark there's a crust, it's tasty, and that's capital-T Tender. Several customers said it was better than in Austin.

GUY ASIDE

When I got the rundown about this place I had my reservations. These guys weren't from the restaurant business. They'd gone and studied barbecue, then opened the place. But I got there and I gotta tell you, it's one of the best barbecue joints I've ever seen. Their energy and attitude and love for barbecue—I mean they were closet barbecueaholics that finally came to recognition. I think they have a fan club now.

He does the baby backs the way Chicago likes them, but also the bigger, meatier St. Louis cut, which he prefers. And now, lots of people are agreeing with him. He puts a thin coating of rub on the back and a thicker coating on the top—so you can barely see the meat through it. There's a beautiful smoke ring on the meat, and it comes off the bone clean. That's a good rib.

You've got a choice of sauce, too: Memphis style with a little more molasses, sweeter; or western North Carolina sauce that's tomato-based with a healthy dose of vinegar in it, so it's tangy but also sweet. He adds Coca-Cola for sweetness and flavor. That I could just drink, and I did, like a fine wine.

For sides they've got mac and cheese, homemade slaw, and baked beans that have a little bit of everything: brown sugar, Worcestershire, liquid smoke, yellow mustard, and chopped beef brisket, then they add some of that Carolina barbecue sauce and some thick-cut onion. And these beans don't go stovetop, they get cooked in the smoker. The caramelization is awesome. That's more than a side, it's like a meal: big flavor.

It's a joint full of big flavors from all over the country—a kind of barbecue fusion, all done up in smoque.

Those beans are da bomb!

Smoque BBQ Mac and Cheese

ADAPTED FROM A RECIPE COURTESY OF SMOQUE

As one regular put it, this mac and cheese is money.

8 SERVINGS

1 pound elbow macaroni

2½ cups evaporated milk

2 large eggs

½ teaspoon dry mustard

¼ teaspoon Louisiana Hot Sauce

¼ teaspoon onion salt

1 teaspoon celery salt

10 ounces or 1¼ cups shredded Cheddar cheese

4 tablespoons (½ stick) unsalted butter

¼ cup bread crumbs

¼ cup grated Parmesan cheese

The great Chicago Food Race . . . loser buys!

1. Bring a large pot of salted water to a boil over high heat. Add the pasta and cook, stirring occasionally, until al dente. Drain.

2. Preheat the broiler.

3. In a large mixing bowl, whisk together the evaporated milk, eggs, dry mustard, hot sauce, and onion and celery salts. Fold in the pasta and about three quarters of the Cheddar cheese.

4. Put the macaroni and cheese mixture back into the pot and cook over medium heat, stirring constantly until the cheese melts and the sauce gets thick. Pour the mac and cheese into a 9 by 13-inch greased casserole.

5. Melt the butter in a skillet over medium heat, add the bread crumbs, and stir to combine. Sprinkle the Parmesan, buttered bread crumbs, and remaining Cheddar over the top of the mac and cheese. Place under the broiler and cook until the top gets a nice golden brown, about 3 minutes. Serve.

South Side Soda Shop and Diner

EST. 1940S, RE-EST. 1986 ★ HOME COOKING IN A CLASSIC CAR

Here in Goshen, Indiana, about thirty miles south of South Bend—you know, the home of Notre Dame University—you'll come across a killer retro-ride truck parked outside a soda shop on South Main. That is, it's part soda shop and part diner.

They're serving up nostalgia that's maybe even better than the original. Down in the basement, owner and chef Nick Boyd makes up a specialty chili one pot at a time. It won the Michiana cook-off seven times. The year they didn't win they didn't vote and lost by one vote. (That'll teach them!)

Boyd starts the chili with ground beef and chopped celery, onion, and green pepper; then he combines pureed tomatoes with chili powder, cumin, and a special secret spice and adds it to the beef along with kidney beans. That simmers for about an hour or hour and a half. You can order it by the sundae-glass-full over egg noodles with chopped onions, shredded cheese, a dollop of sour cream, and a parsley sprig on top. That's named, for no particular reason, for Nick's hometown: a Philly Chili. It's a home run. I could get that by the bucket.

> We received an e-mail from a soldier in Iraq wanting our chili recipe. *DD&D* has really reminded people of the good homemade food served at mom-and-pop restaurants.
>
> —CHARITY BOYD, SOUTH SIDE SODA SHOP AND DINER

Not bad from a guy who never dreamed he'd be cooking for anybody. Nick and his wife, Charity, were antique dealers when her father asked them to help him open his restaurant. Two years later they owned it, and two decades later they've become a local institution. Nicole Boyd has been waiting tables since she was three, so some customers have known her for her whole life.

They serve hand-chopped cheese steaks with Swiss-American cheese that adds a little bite, fresh-made spiral fries, and family recipes like the grilled liverwurst, bacon, and onion sandwich that Charity's grandfather just had to have. In other words, they make things they want to eat, says Nick, like a New England seafood feast of mussels and clams for a Friday-night seafood special. Don't miss his orange-peel-flavored fresh-baked bread, plus fifty types of pies (the lemon meringue won the Indiana Pie Quest Contest) and colorful retro ice cream floats like the old-fashioned Green River, which harks back to days of old. Nicole and I took a shot of that green syrup straight and man, it was like liquid LifeSavers. So okay, you might want to steer clear of Green River shooters, but folks keep coming back for more floats, sundaes, and surprising diner and non-diner delights that taste like home.

SODA SHOP HISTORY

Built in the early 1900s, the building the diner is in was originally a grocery store. In the 1940s the Bastian Blessings soda fountain was installed where it still remains, serving up the sodas, shakes, malts, and floats. The Boyds started restoration work in 1985 and reopened in 1986, having polished and spiffed the place to its original glory. They added the 1950s dining car in 1993 for additional seating, and to add to their already retro feel.

Built in the early 1900s, the South Side Soda Shop was once a grocery store. Now, in 2008, they cook the groceries for you.

Mom's Meatloaf

ADAPTED FROM A RECIPE COURTESY OF CHARITY BOYD OF SOUTH SIDE SODA SHOP AND DINER

Try another savory taste of home, in true diner fashion.

4 SERVINGS

1 egg

2 teaspoons Worcestershire sauce

2 teaspoons prepared horseradish

1 teaspoon dry mustard

½ teaspoon salt

½ teaspoon freshly ground black pepper

½ onion, very finely chopped

1 pound ground beef

¾ cup bread crumbs

¾ cup ketchup

1. Preheat the oven to 350°F.

2. In a large bowl, mix together the egg, 3 tablespoons water, the Worcestershire, horseradish, mustard, salt, pepper, and onion. Add the beef and bread crumbs and use your hands to quickly and thoroughly combine. Gently press the mixture into a 1.5-quart glass (Pyrex) loaf pan. Spread the ketchup over the top and bake for 45 to 50 minutes.

The green river runs through it.

Triple XXX Family Restaurant

EST. 1929 ★ ON THE HILL . . . BUT ON THE LEVEL

. . . .

★ TRACK IT DOWN ★
. . . .

2 N. Salisbury Street
West Lafayette, IN 47906
765-743-5373
www.triplexxxfamilyrestaurant.com

I'm here in West Lafayette, Indiana, the home of Purdue University, and two things come to mind: one, how did the Boilermakers really get their name and two, what in the world would they be serving at a place called the Triple XXX Family Restaurant?

One answer is burgers, burgers, and burgers. And the other might have to do with the university's fame for engineering instruction in the 1800s. As for the fame of their athletes, it's a local obsession: just check out the photos of football stars plastered on the walls of the Triple XXX. They even have burgers named after former players, like the Bernie Flowers All-Pro.

Owners Greg and Carrie Ehresman are committed to keeping this place the iconic institution it's been for more than seventy-five years. First off, the hamburgers are called chop steaks. See, the burgers start with steak, cut and ground fresh right here. It's not just any steak, either; it's top choice sirloin butt. Their Hollymatic Super 54 then turns the meat into patties. This machine was made in 1954, by the way, and it sounds as old as it looks, but it gets the job done. The secret to their burgers is totally outta bounds. You take the poker-chip-shaped patty, roll it in flour, then smash it down flat. They're then placed on the grill with just a touch of oil.

Greg remembers sitting up at the counter when he was little, watching his dad order a big fat double cheeseburger and wishing he could have one. So it was a coming of age moment when he could. One day, the cook at the time, Barney, decided it was time. So he made it for Greg, brought it out himself, and just looked at him with a big grin on his face and said, "There you go." And that's a good way to start eating burgers.

Barney himself wasn't a double-cheese guy, so if you order the Barney burger you're getting onions and cheese. He liked a thick-cut raw white onion, but most people can't handle that, so the cooks grill the onions. Or you can have a burger with your breakfast alongside two fried eggs and fried potatoes with gravy; that's a Drew Breeze Special.

They'll top their burgers with just about anything: check out the Duane Purvis All-American, a sirloin cheeseburger with onion, pickles, lettuce, and tomatoes on a toasted bun with a thick spread of peanut butter. Greg loves it, but Carrie doesn't care for it. It's a love-hate kinda situation. Greg envied me my first bite. But me, I wanted my mommy.

Greg also makes a pork tenderloin sandwich that's pounded, grilled up just like the burger, and simply served on a toasted bun. Ya gotta try this bad boy.

The Camaro is right behind the stand. You just can't see it.

Triple XXX Family Restaurant Potato Salad

ADAPTED FROM A RECIPE COURTESY OF GREG EHRESMAN OF TRIPLE XXX FAMILY RESTAURANT

Just like everything at Triple XXX, they do it old-school, and this potato salad is no exception—as all-American as it gets.

6 SERVINGS

4 medium Idaho russet potatoes, scrubbed

Salt and freshly ground black pepper

3 hard-boiled eggs, peeled

3½ tablespoons mayonnaise (recommended: Miracle Whip)

1½ teaspoons yellow mustard

2 teaspoons sweet relish

½ cup chopped onion, such as white or Vidalia

1. Put the potatoes in a large pot, cover with cold water, and season with salt. Bring to a boil over high heat, and cook until the potatoes can be easily pierced with a small knife or fork, about 20 minutes. Drain and run under cold running water. When cool enough to handle, peel and cut the potatoes into equal bite-size pieces.

2. Place each egg in an egg cutter. Slice it once, turn it 90 degrees, and slice again. Repeat with the other eggs. (You can also use a knife and thinly slice the eggs.) Set aside.

3. Mix the mayonnaise, mustard, relish, and onion together in large bowl. Season with salt and pepper to taste. Gently fold the potatoes into the mayonnaise mixture, being careful not to smash them while you mix. Add the eggs to the bowl and fold lightly. Refrigerate for a couple of hours or overnight to bring the flavors together. Serve.

Triple XXX Family Restaurant
Famous Root Beer Frost

ADAPTED FROM A RECIPE COURTESY OF GREG EHRESMAN

Greg's father, Jack, has been drinking root beer frosts since 1935, when he turned five years old; Greg has also been drinking frosts since he was old enough to sit on a Triple XXX bar stool. Greg and Carrie's daughter, Samantha, continues the family tradition of drinking a root beer frost with her chopped steak sandwich whenever she's in the restaurant.

1 SERVING

2 scoops premium vanilla ice cream

6 to 8 ounces Triple XXX Root Beer (more or less, depending how thick you like it)

1. Put the ice cream and root beer in a blender and blend to make a thick, but still chunky, shake. Pour into a frosted mug and enjoy.

This is an embroidered patch from . . . a restaurant. Really—a restaurant.

Joe's Gizzard City

EST. 1960 ★ THE BEST PLUCKIN' GIZZARD IN THE WORLD

★ TRACK IT DOWN ★

**120 W. Main Street
Potterville, MI 48876
517-645-2120
www.gizzardcity.com**

When you're ordering fried chicken you're usually asked, "Breast, thigh, drumstick, or wing?" But in Potterville they ask, "How do you want your gizzards?" Joe's Gizzard City is truly one of a kind.

I told the owner, Joe Bristol Jr., that if he said gizzards tasted like chicken, I was leaving. He said, "This is the place you want to try it. Everywhere else it's gonna taste like you bit into your tennis shoe, or your belt." Apparently, alligators and earthworms also have gizzards, so I considered myself lucky.

The story goes that when Joe Bristol Sr. took over his father's chicken joint in 1968, he didn't want to waste a thing, not even the gizzards. "And it became quite a deal," he says—which is a big understatement. Joe Jr. took the restaurant over from his father after doing the corporate restaurant route for a few years, and now he's the muscle of the restaurant. Speaking of muscles, the gizzard is the second stomach: It's not the "working" part of the stomach, but the muscle of it.

So I take one look at a tray of raw gizzards and say, "That's gnarly." But I'm in. They first have to pressure-cook the gizzards to tenderize them. (This is why most people don't eat gizzards at home.) They're cooked with garlic powder, celery salt, and salt. Next is a toss with Joe's famous flour mix—a "special flour" they won't give up that has a cornstarch consistency. Then they fry them up. You know what, I think they're not bad. The seasoning that they pressure-cook them in is great, and the batter is on point. Deep-fried isn't your only option: they've got naked, Cajun, garlic-and-herb, and even a gizzard omelet.

Everywhere I go now I get noticed for being on the show. Thanks a lot! Now I have to behave!

—JOE BRISTOL II,
JOE'S GIZZARD CITY

There's plenty more on the menu: burgers, massive fish and fries, and even deep-fried desserts. But their fried chicken is what originally got the place going. Joe Jr. learned to make it from his grandmother. They first boil the chicken with garlic powder and celery salt, then coat it with batter and fry it—all in the name of moist chicken. It's super tender and has a great hit of garlic. It sure is different, and they're big on different here. They do deep-fried hot dogs with melted cheese, deep-fried Oreos, even deep-fried Twinkies they call Frinkies. Now, that might be illegal to serve—it's freaky.

But if you want something really freaky, how about a deep-fried burger? They coat the patty in batter, fry it, and place it between buns. It's crunchy on the outside, soft and juicy on the inside, and I like it better than the regular burger. But why stop there? I got into the spirit of the place and battered an entire cheeseburger—bun and all—and deep-fried it up. It was the first time that feat was ever performed at Gizzard City. I'm not kidding you, it's money. Joe's put it on the menu as the Triple D Burger, and I hear it's been selling like crazy. I'll order one of those every time I stop in—along with a gizzard appetizer and a freaky fried dessert.

Get your gizzard fix off Route 66. This place is a trip. (I'd take that as a compliment, Joe.)

"Joe, I'll arm-wrestle ya for *those* gizzards?"
"Bring it, Guido."

The Triple D Burger

ADAPTED FROM A RECIPE COURTESY OF JOE'S GIZZARD CITY

Yeah, you too can make culinary history in a deep-fryer.

MAKES 4 BURGERS

2½ cups batter mix (recommended: Joe's Famous Batter Mix at www.gizzardcity.com)

Oil, for frying

1⅓ pounds 85% lean ground chuck

Kosher salt and freshly ground black pepper

4 (4-inch) hamburger buns

8 slices American cheese

½ cup chopped white onion

4 tomato slices

16 slices hamburger pickles

Condiments of your choice

1. Grab a medium mixing bowl and a whisk. Put 1¼ cups cold water in the bowl and add the batter mix. Whisk together to make a batter that's a little thicker than pancake batter.

2. Heat a deep-fryer, or about 6 inches of oil in a large deep, heavy-bottomed pot, until a deep-fry thermometer reads 375°F. Line a plate with paper towels.

3. Shape the ground chuck into 4 even patties. Season with salt and pepper to taste. Heat a skillet or flat-top grill to medium-high. Cook the burgers to medium-rare or to your desired degree of doneness.

4. Open the hamburger buns and set a piece of cheese on each side of the open buns. Sprinkle onion on all the bottoms and lay a tomato on all the tops of the buns. Top the tomatoes with 4 pickle slices. Gently place the cooked burger on the bottom, close the buns, and smash the buns together. The tighter the better!

5. Hold each hamburger together and dip into the batter to completely cover it. Carefully drop it into the oil and fry until the coating crisps and turns golden brown, 4 to 5 minutes. Drain on the paper towels and serve. Repeat with the remaining burgers.

6. Serve with desired condiments.

That is one huge cock-a-doodle-doo.

The Fly Trap

EST. 2004 ★ A FINER DINER

I grew up in the great town of Ferndale, California, which is exactly 2,433 miles away from Ferndale, Michigan—which is home to the Fly Trap. They call themselves "a finer diner," and their approach to diner food is off the hook. It's different, fun, cool, and inexpensive—and it may be the only time you'll see tofu on *DD&D*.

Restaurant vets Gavin McMillian and Kara McClanaghan, and Kara's unsuspecting brother Sean, have taken the idea of a classic diner and are doing it their way. (Sean says he got suckered in: they needed a dishwasher.)

When they first got in there, it really was a fly trap. But they learned how to swing a hammer, and threw it together. The menu's heavy on Asian foods, which Gavin has loved since his

days in college when he had a Japanese-American roommate. "I'd go over to his mom's house," says Gavin, "and get free food, basically. It kind of piqued my interest in it." These days he's cooking Asian cuisine from all over the map, from tofu fried rice with roasted mushrooms, peppers, and eggplant to Thai-style spicy peanut chicken and a favorite Vietnamese soup called pho. That's "ph" pronounced like fat, and it's a fat dish, as Gavin says. With a rich, roasted-vegetable-with-a-kick stock, noodles, and seared tofu, it was too beautiful to eat in the kitchen. It rates up with some of the best bowls I've had. Definitely check out the recipe on page 140; Gavin's a maniac.

Even the less exotic dishes here get a Fly Trap spin. He's got beets in the corned beef hash, and gingerbread waffles with homemade syrup, fresh apple, and Michigan cherries. And then, I read it to my kids, so I had to see the Scrambled Green Eggs and Ham. There's a poblano pesto, Jack cheese, and seared slabs of ham. Tell me that's not a festival of flavor.

They've also got green burgers made with spinach and feta and a salmon burger. He does a rough chop of the fresh salmon before throwing it in the blender with sambal (an Asian chili-garlic sauce), scallions, and black sesame seeds. Give it a pulse and they're ready to make patties. No binder needed. He sears it up on the grill, then puts it on a toasted bun with a little lime aioli and a few slices of cucumber, tomato, and red onion. That's tasty—but what I really dig are the sesame seeds.

Good prices, good food, good people—this is what a diner is meant to be.

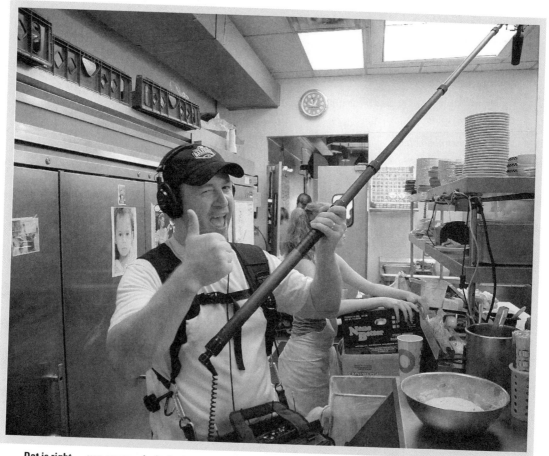

Dat is right . . . you are now in da Arnie workout program.

Lemongrass Pho Bowl

ADAPTED FROM A RECIPE COURTESY OF GAVIN MCMILLIAN OF THE FLY TRAP

NOTE: Gavin's original recipe calls for "Dragon" noodles, fresh ramen, lo mein, or buckwheat noodles. We used buckwheat noodles. The weights and package sizes of other kinds may vary.

8 SERVINGS

Soup

1 pound cremini mushrooms, roughly chopped

2 carrots, diced

1 yellow onion, diced

2 celery stalks, diced

2 thumb-size pieces of peeled fresh ginger, diced

1 lemongrass stalk, pounded with the back of knife, then roughly chopped

¼ cup canola oil, divided

½ bunch of fresh cilantro, leaves roughly chopped

1 bunch of sweet basil, leaves roughly chopped

1 to 3 jalapeño peppers, roughly chopped

½ cup soy sauce

2 heaping tablespoons sambal oelek

1 tablespoon toasted sesame oil

Kosher salt and freshly ground black pepper

1 small eggplant, diced

1 red bell pepper, stemmed, seeded, and diced

¼ pound shiitake mushrooms, sliced

¼ pound snow peas, sliced

1 (11-ounce) package buckwheat noodles (soba)

1½ pounds fresh spinach, stemmed

Tofu (optional)

Spicy Vinaigrette

¼ cup sambal oelek

¼ cup soy sauce

¼ cup apple cider vinegar

2 tablespoons dark brown sugar

1 teaspoon toasted sesame oil

1 cucumber, diced

3 radishes, sliced

2 cups mung beans

Lime wedges

1. Preheat the oven to 350°F.

2. For the soup: Put the cremini mushrooms, half the carrots, onion, celery, ginger, and lemongrass in a roasting pan and toss with 2 to 3 tablespoons of the canola oil. Roast until tender, about 25 minutes. Transfer the vegetables to a large soup pot; add 1 gallon cool water and bring to a simmer over medium-high heat. Add the cilantro, basil, and jalapeños and continue to simmer for 20 minutes. Strain and reserve the broth. Add the soy sauce, sambal oelek, sesame oil, and salt and pepper to taste. (The base for the soup can be prepared ahead.)

3. When ready to serve, spread the eggplant, the remaining carrots, the bell pepper, shiitake mushrooms, and snow peas out on a rimmed baking sheet. Toss with the remaining oil. Roast until cooked through, 8 to 10 minutes.

4. Bring the soup to a boil; add the roasted vegetables and the noodles and cook until just tender. Add spinach and tofu, if desired.

5. For the vinaigrette: Whisk together the sambal oelek, soy sauce, cider vinegar, dark brown sugar, and sesame oil in a medium bowl. Toss in the cucumber, radishes, and mung beans.

6. To assemble the pho: Divide the noodles evenly among 8 large bowls. Pour the broth with roasted vegetables over the noodles and top with the spicy vinaigrette. Serve with lime wedges.

Al's Breakfast

EST. 1950 ★ DINKYTOWN'S JAMES BEARD AWARD WINNER

One of the best things about *Diners, Drive-Ins and Dives* is that you can't judge a book by its cover. Take this breakfast place in Minneapolis. It was built in an alley between two buildings—the owner corrected me, it's a dump aspiring to be a dive—in an area called Dinkytown. And would you believe, it's a James Beard Award winner?

★ TRACK IT DOWN ★

413 14th Avenue, SE
Minneapolis, MN 55414
612-331-9991

They're yelling back and forth at each other, the wall behind the stools is worn out from people waiting in line there . . . and then there's the food. The omelets are beautiful; the eggs Benedict are served with real hollandaise; they serve fluffy scrambled eggs with Cheddar cheese, mushroom, and garlic; and everything's made fresh and to order. There are two kinds of pancake batter: buttermilk and whole wheat with honey. Their corned beef hash is money, made with onions, green pepper, garlic, parsley, and a hint of horseradish. Owner Doug Grina loves food and it shows. He says he goes home from here sometime after one PM, stops at the grocery, sees what looks good, and plans a dinner for that night.

In 2004 Al's Breakfast received a James Beard Award for being an American classic. (Doug says that the award helps in making the leap from a dump to a dive.) The original owner, Al, started the place in 1950 and retired in 1974, and Doug and James Brandes continued the tradition in 1979. The setup hasn't changed in years, with the grill up front and omelets and scrambles in back by the water heater. He refused my offer of a twenty-dollar Radio Shack intercom system as he yelled, "Three eggs huevos on an oval!"—Doug's got some lungs on him. "What do I need that for!"

Don't blink or you'll drive by it—I did, twice!

They have a spring scrambled special with asparagus—which Doug said was pre-NAFTA, so now you can get asparagus whenever you want it. The summer special has basil and mozzarella, and the winter special has spinach, feta, and tomatoes. Greg admits after that the naming system became somewhat obscure. Which means feel free to order the winter in the spring. As one regular says, it's winter somewhere.

Then there's the Jose, named after a customer. That's two poached eggs, salsa, and Cheddar cheese on top of hash browns fried with soy bean oil—for $5.25. Doug doesn't like to raise prices—or paint the place, or throw anything out, or change anything. No credit cards here; instead they've got payment books that date back to the 1960s. Here's how it works: you put cash onto your account and they keep track as you eat, backward to zero.

Neither of these cats is Al. The dude on the left is Doug Grina and the one on the right is Jim Brandes.

Buttermilk Pancakes

ADAPTED FROM A RECIPE COURTESY OF JAMES BRANDES
AND DOUGLAS GRINA, OWNERS OF AL'S BREAKFAST

Doug says the recipe is not nearly as important as being able to feel your batter and know what's going on with it. Sometimes he has to add buttermilk, sometimes some flour—it's never exactly the same.

MAKES 2 DOZEN PANCAKES

3 cups all-purpose flour

1 tablespoon plus 1 teaspoon baking powder

2 teaspoons sugar

1 teaspoon baking soda

1 teaspoon kosher salt

1 quart buttermilk

2 eggs, beaten

6 tablespoons (¾ stick) unsalted butter, melted

**Wild Maine blueberries
    (optional; available frozen)**

Vegetable oil or butter, for the griddle

1. Whisk the dry ingredients together in a medium bowl. In a large bowl, whisk the buttermilk with the eggs, then whisk in the dry mix. Whisk in the melted butter. Gently stir in the blueberries, if using.

2. Heat a stovetop griddle over medium heat, or an electric griddle to 375°F. Brush with oil or add some butter and melt. Ladle about ¼ cup of the batter onto the griddle per pancake, leaving space for the pancakes to spread without touching. Flip the pancakes when bubbles break the surface and cook until golden brown on the second side, adjusting the heat as necessary to keep them from browning too quickly.

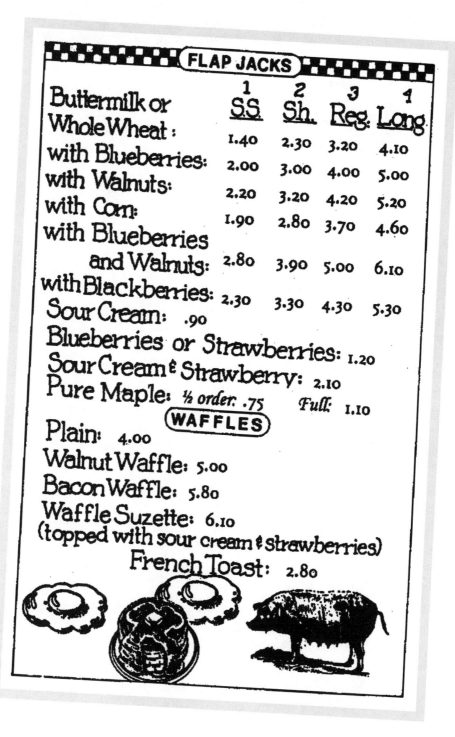

FLAP JACKS

	1 S.S.	2 Sh.	3 Reg.	1 Long
Buttermilk or Whole Wheat:	1.40	2.30	3.20	4.10
with Blueberries:	2.00	3.00	4.00	5.00
with Walnuts:	2.20	3.20	4.20	5.20
with Corn:	1.90	2.80	3.70	4.60
with Blueberries and Walnuts:	2.80	3.90	5.00	6.10
with Blackberries:	2.30	3.30	4.30	5.30

Sour Cream: .90
Blueberries or Strawberries: 1.20
Sour Cream & Strawberry: 2.10
Pure Maple: ½ order .75   Full: 1.10

WAFFLES

Plain: 4.00
Walnut Waffle: 5.00
Bacon Waffle: 5.80
Waffle Suzette: 6.10
(topped with sour cream & strawberries)
French Toast: 2.80

Psycho Suzi's

EST. 2003 ★ THE POOR MAN'S PARADISE

★ TRACK IT DOWN ★

2519 Marshall Street NE
Minneapolis, MN 55418
612-788-9069
www.psychosuzis.com

I dig funk joints that have funky names 'cause it usually means they serve funky food, so I think I found in Psycho Suzi's Motor Lounge, aka the "poor man's paradise," my Minneapolis hang-out. It's a one-of-a-kind tiki lounge. This is an experience I was told I needed to check out in an e-mail from viewer Cindi Maxham. She says, "We're classy trashy."

They've got one of the most out-of-bounds menus folks have ever fallen in love with. For example, the retro pot luck pickle roll-up is a pickle rolled in salami and cream cheese and sliced, and they've got deviled eggs or tater tots. But they've also got totally custom pizzas, flaming tiki drinks, and deep-fried everything—as in beer-battered asparagus.

Where does all this funkiness originate? From the mind of clothing-designer-turned-tattoo artist-turned-restaurateur Leslie Bock. "I decided I needed a restaurant and a bar just to mix it up," she says. "I'm not known to be the most sensible person." So four years ago she snapped up an old A&W drive-in and turned it tiki.

Best-sellers here are anything beer-battered, and the pizza. The batter is flour, baking soda, salt, beaten eggs, and Pabst Blue Ribbon. It goes great on something called a cheese curd, and people here say they're a state-fair favorite. I'd never heard of them before. Apparently, they're white Cheddar from Wisconsin. The batter's money, and the curds taste like mozzarella. Red Rockets are beer-battered mini wieners that are hand-dipped and come with mustard, but there are also beer-battered onion rings, hot wings, even Snickers bars and something called a mini Mex roll. The recipe for the Mex roll came out of Leslie's creative head, and it defies description, so she's provided the recipe on page 148.

All the tiki cups in the place were collected by Leslie at tiki conventions. What to enjoy in your tiki cup? You can order gin, tequila, vodka, Triple Sec; rum with mango, orange, and pineapple; a float of dark rum; and a lit volcano of Bacardi 151 rum. Yeah, that'll light you up. But rum isn't restricted to the cocktails at this joint. Consider the Paradise City Pizza Pie with rum-soaked raisins: they're soaked in pineapple schnapps and coconut rum and combined with Leslie's homemade red sauce, Canadian bacon, pineapple, and red onion, with a final layer of mozzarella, Romano, and oregano. It's really good pie. They've got thirteen types of pizza that rock, like the thin-crust white wine–garlic sauce pie with artichokes and tomatoes or the grilled chicken pizza with spicy barbecue sauce. She is also doing a deep-dish with sun-dried tomatoes and goat cheese that's probably the best deep-dish I've had in the last ten years.

Bottom line: Leslie knows no boundaries. She's the melting pot of melting pots. Every walk of life comes here, and there's a party going on all the time.

Reminds me of the *Brady Bunch* tiki head.

Mini Mex Rolls

ADAPTED FROM A RECIPE COURTESY OF LESLIE BOCK OF PSYCHO SUZI'S

These are crazy tasty.

MAKES ABOUT 16 ROLLS

1 cooked chicken breast, finely chopped

¼ cup taco seasoning

1½ cups shredded pepper Jack cheese

½ cup diced roasted red pepper, drained

½ cup chopped pickled jalapeño peppers, drained

½ cup corn kernels

½ cup cooked black beans, rinsed and well drained

1 scallion, chopped

Kosher salt and freshly ground black pepper

Canola oil, for frying

1 large egg

About 16 spring roll wrappers

1. Heat the chicken, taco seasoning, and ½ cup water in a skillet over medium heat until the liquid thickens and is fully absorbed into the chicken, about 4 minutes.

2. Combine the cheese, red pepper, and jalapeño in a blender until finely chopped. Transfer to a bowl and stir in the corn, beans, scallion, and the chicken mixture. Season with salt and pepper to taste.

3. Heat 2 inches of oil in a heavy-bottomed pot until a deep-fry thermometer reads 375°F. While the oil heats, make the rolls. Whisk together the egg and 2 tablespoons water. Lay a spring roll wrapper on a clean work surface and brush the outer edges with the egg mixture. Spoon 2 heaping

tablespoons of the Mex mixture onto the lower part of the wrapper and spread it into a log shape. Fold the wrapper over the ends of the filling, then roll up and seal. Repeat with all the filling and wrappers.

4. Line a plate with paper towels. Deep-fry the mini Mex rolls until they turn golden brown and rise to the surface, 2 to 3 minutes. Remove from the oil and drain on the paper towels. Cool slightly and serve.

North Shore? . . . Oh! The North Shore of Minneapolis—I get it!

Iron Barley

EST. 2003 ★ A NEIGHBORHOOD GOURMET TAVERN

★ TRACK IT DOWN ★

**5510 Virginia Avenue
St. Louis, MO 63111
314-351-4500
www.ironbarley.com**

In the southernmost part of St. Louis, about a quarter mile from the Mississippi River, is Dutch Town, a neighborhood loaded with brick two-story flats and home to this neighborhood favorite.

His restaurant might look like a corner tavern, but this guy's cooking up pork scaloppini and fresh mussels with leeks and cream. And the namesake grain, barley, shows up all over the menu, as in the barley salad or the seafood barley paella. "It's not your average pub grub, that's for sure," says owner Tom Coghill. Running a gourmet tavern wasn't what he planned to do. He worked the whole hotel circuit "chasing the starched jacket," as he says. No headband like he's wearing now; it was black-jacket-and-checked-pants land. But after years as a chef in upscale restaurants all across St. Louis, he took a gamble and bought this place, and he's cranking out whatever he feels like from just about everywhere—like a Spanish seafood stew called zarzuela. You could put the seasonings for this stew on a flip-flop and it would taste good. But he takes care with the fish, and it's no rubbery experience.

He also makes German spaetzle (a tiny pasta) served with schnitzel. He pounds a two-ounce slice of pork tenderloin thin, flours it, dips it in egg wash, then in bread crumbs, and seasons it in the skillet with salt, pepper, and granulated garlic. When it's brown he tosses some white wine in there, flames it up, and swirls in a pat of maître d'hôtel butter (which has lemon, garlic, and parsley mixed in) right before serving. That's all he needs to have on the menu, in my opinion—it's that good!

On the downscale side, he makes a Ballistic Elvis Sandwich. He takes two slices of thick-cut Texas toast, chunky peanut butter, strawberry jam, and American cheese, with a sprinkle of crushed red pepper—that's the ballistic part. Then he tops all that with a halved and grilled banana, slaps it together on the grill, and it's there: a cholesterol fiend's dream.

And he also does his own oak-roasted pork, on a home-built smoker. Everything on it came off of a semi—one piece was a gas tank, one was an oil tank—no kidding around. And he's got his own way of prepping the meat: butchering it with a power saw. Yes, a power saw. Then he ties it up to do a nice round eye and spreads on a rub with more than a dozen seasonings, including cayenne, brown sugar, coriander, and ginger. It's served in a cast-iron skillet on a bed of toasted barley and grilled vegetables. He's got this down to a science.

The drive-in movie theater tomato.

Zarzuela

ADAPTED FROM A RECIPE COURTESY OF TOM COGHILL OF IRON BARLEY

Enjoy—it's kind of like a cross between a cioppino and a bouillabaisse, with a little more spice.

4 TO 6 SERVINGS

¼ cup olive oil

4 garlic cloves, chopped

1 large yellow onion, diced

1 large green bell pepper, stemmed, seeded, and diced

¼ teaspoon dried thyme

¼ teaspoon dried marjoram

¼ teaspoon crushed red pepper flakes

2 or 3 bay leaves

1 teaspoon kosher salt

¼ teaspoon freshly ground black pepper

1 tablespoon chili powder, or to taste

¼ teaspoon saffron threads

1 cup white wine

1 cup chicken broth

1 (14.5-ounce) can diced tomatoes

¼ cup Spanish brandy (optional)

1 pound firm fish chunks, such as swordfish, shark, or halibut

8 to 12 medium shrimp, cleaned

12 to 18 mussels, scrubbed

8 to 12 littleneck clams, scrubbed

½ cup pitted kalamata olives

½ pound squid, cleaned and cut into rings

1. Heat the oil in a large pot over medium-high heat. Add the garlic and cook until fragrant, taking care that it doesn't brown or it'll get bitter. Add the onion and bell pepper and continue to cook until translucent, about 3 minutes. Add the thyme, marjoram, red pepper flakes, bay leaves, salt, and pepper and cook for 2 to 3 minutes. Add the chili powder to taste and saffron, stir, and cook for 30 seconds to open up their flavors.

2. Add the wine and chicken broth and bring to a boil, stirring constantly. Add the tomatoes and brandy, if using, and bring to a boil. Simmer for a couple of minutes to bring the flavors together.

3. Add the fish, shrimp, mussels, and clams and stir. Bring to a boil and simmer just until the clams open. Turn off the heat and add the olives and squid, stir, and let stand a few minutes to cook the squid. Remove and discard the bay leaves and any mussels or clams that have not opened. Serve.

YJ's Snack Bar

EST. 1928, RE-EST. 1997 ★ A THIRD-WORLD SNACK BAR

. . . .

★ TRACK IT DOWN ★
. . . .
128 W. 18th Street
Kansas City, MO 64108
816-472-5533

This is a great example of what we say on *Triple D*: if it's funky, we'll find it. Check out what we found in Kansas City.

Owner David Ford says, "We get referred to as a third-world snack bar." Or as one regular puts it: "Like your mom's home cooking, if she were cooking something from Guatemala."

He's dishing it up in a closet-size kitchen with two electric burners and a sidewalk grill. This self-taught cook brought back his favorite dishes from his world travels. He's got an African supplier, a Latin supplier, a Middle Eastern supplier—it's different every day. And the way the food got figured out, David says, is from what he wanted to eat. You've got to check out the chalkboard to know what's cooking.

Some days it's Mayan Tostadas, or North African Lamb Kabobs with Couscous, or Turkish Stuffed Figs, or Mexican-Style Fish in Banana Leaves—wow, that was good. David is an artist who happened to live above the restaurant. It's a shop that had been open since 1928, and when they put a sign in the window that read DELI FOR SALE, David thought, This will be good, figuring he'd put in a cappuccino machine. After all, he recalls, "I was already feeding twenty artists upstairs in my house every week. I could charge them now."

There is no way all these people can't fit in there.

For the Mediterranean plate he stuffs dates with soft cheese, wraps them in aged prosciutto, and heats them on top of chorizo, sizzling in the pan—a recipe straight from Grenada that's great with sherry *or* a cold beer. He serves it with fresh hummus spiced with a hot Asian chile sauce. That warms up on you. Then he throws in a Thai-spiced chicken that's massaged with torn sweet Thai basil leaves, super-spicy hot red chile oil, a touch of sesame oil, a little dried thyme, sesame, and a little turmeric. The breasts are then thrown on the grill till done. And he's putting it all together with pita, olives, fresh feta cheese, and dollops of Middle Eastern yogurt and a traditional hot sauce called harissa. You build as you go, throw it down as you like. Take a tour of that plate and you've really been somewhere.

Now, this doesn't mean that David ignores the down-home style of American food. He also chases big flavors close to home and does a dirty rice that I call a jambalaya. By grilling up the spice-rubbed chicken and Cajun and andouille sausages before adding them in to cook with the rice, man, does he make something tasty, whatever you call it.

Tiny kitchen, big menu, and great handmade, fresh, seasonal food—I like it, total freedom.

YJ's Fish and Banana Leaves

ADAPTED FROM A RECIPE COURTESY OF DAVID FORD OF YJ'S SNACK BAR

David says that you can season as you would like, using any spice rub, and you can get creative with whatever vegetables you want to pack in the banana leaves.

4 SERVINGS

2 banana leaves

Extra-virgin olive oil, for drizzling (rosemary or other infused oil is great here)

1 tablespoon thinly sliced dried orange peels

1 green plantain, peeled and thinly sliced

2 tomatillos, peeled, rinsed, and thinly sliced

Kosher salt and freshly ground black pepper

4 (4-ounce) tilapia fillets

1 lemon, quartered

Tarragon fish rub (optional)

Small handful of pitted olives

1 medium zucchini, thinly sliced

2 bay leaves, halved

1 small red onion, thinly sliced in rings

1 star fruit, thinly sliced

I think the prices have gone up a bit.

1. Preheat the oven to 325°F.

2. Tear the banana leaves in half to make 4 pieces, each about 16 by 10 inches. Drizzle the leaves with the olive oil. Sprinkle some of the orange peels in the center of each banana leaf, then scatter the plantain and tomatillos on top. Season the vegetables lightly with salt and pepper to taste. Place a tilapia fillet on top of the vegetables and squeeze lemon juice over the fish. Sprinkle the rub over the fish, if using, or season with more salt and pepper. Scatter olives around the fish, and then lay the zucchini slices and half a bay leaf on top.

3. Loosely fold the banana leaves around the fish to make 4 packages. Top with the red onion and star fruit. Set the packages in a baking dish and bake 15 minutes. Remove from oven and let package rest for 2 minutes. Let diners unwrap their own package—reminding them to remove the bay leaf before eating.

He can't play the piano from there . . .

Franks Diner

EST. 1926 ★ HOME OF THE GARBAGE PLATE

Here in Kenosha, Wisconsin, about an hour north of Chicago and just a few blocks off of Lake Michigan, there's a place where the breakfast special's called a Garbage Plate. The "half" portion of the Plate looks like a full, and even then you may have something leftover for the doggy bag. But they're cooking all sorts of other great things, from fluffy scrambles with a huge slab of ham to pancakes with peanut butter, a Reuben omelet with Thousand Island dressing, and French toast made from fresh cinnamon rolls.

> ★ TRACK IT DOWN ★
>
> **508 58th Street**
> **Kenosha, WI 53140**
> **262-657-1017**
> **www.franksdinerkenosha.com**

At Franks Diner, there are a lot of people in a little place, and they've been packing them in for just about forever. The diner was pulled to the site by a team of six horses. The original owner Anthony Franks's kids, Joanne and Donald, have been telling the story for years. They say it was a big event when it came to town; the street was full of people waiting for this strange car to come to Kenosha—straight from the Jerry O'Mahoney company in New Jersey. Anthony had seen an ad in the paper and paid $7,500 plus $325 shipping to get his business started. He added a dining room in 1935 and a larger kitchen in the mid-1940s. The Frankses ran it until 2001, when Lynn Groleau and Chris Schwartz took it over.

Chris and Lynn had no experience in the food biz. They kept the name 'cause it's part of history, and they were regulars already. When they heard it was for sale, they thought, let's go look at it, and a couple bottles of wine later, it was a done deal. Donald says his father would be proud of what they've accomplished. Honestly, they look like seasoned line cooks now.

GUY ASIDE

These girls are crazy. Their gag line is, "Order what you want, eat what you get." Love that, so off da hook. They're working the line themselves, and it's a real tribute to why they're doing so well in their business.

The famous Garbage Plate is the number-one heavy hitter here. It's a hunk of hash browns, with whatever's in the kitchen scrambled up with eggs, for $8.95. But they all start the same way: hash browns, onions, green bell pepper, and chorizo. It's really good, and I'm not even the hugest fan of eggs. And they scratch-bake everything here, even the bread for the French toast.

This is one of those places where everybody knows your name, and it's been that way for eight decades, which makes Franks the oldest continuously operating lunch car diner in the Midwest.

Food science at Franks.

Chorizo Garbage Plate

ADAPTED FROM A RECIPE COURTESY OF CHRIS SCHWARTZ, CO-OWNER OF FRANKS DINER

This is the basic recipe, but you can add bacon, ham, or sausage, or make it veggie with zucchini and mushrooms and minus the chorizo.

3 LARGE SERVINGS (OR 1 AT FRANKS)

2 to 3 tablespoons vegetable oil

2 cups prepared hash browns or shredded cooked potatoes

½ cup diced onion

½ cup diced green bell pepper

1 tablespoon seeded and diced jalapeño (optional)

1 cup diced or ground cooked chorizo

½ cup diced tomato

5 large eggs, lightly beaten with salt to taste

½ cup shredded Cheddar cheese

Toast or tortillas, for serving

1. Preheat a flat griddle or a large nonstick skillet over medium-high heat. Add the oil and place 3 heaping handfuls of the potatoes on the grill or skillet. Top with the onion, green pepper, jalapeño, if using, and chorizo. Mix together slightly. Cook until the potatoes brown slightly, about 4 minutes, then flip the mixture and cook to brown the other side, about 4 minutes more. Add the tomato and eggs. Mix the eggs into the potatoes and cook, flipping once, until the eggs set, another 2 to 3 minutes. Add the cheese and cook until slightly melted. Mix the hash together to distribute cheese and tomato throughout.

2. Serve with toast or tortillas.

All aboard the order-what-you-want, eat-what-you-get express!

Chino Bandido

EST. 1990 ★ FEAST ON THE BORDER OF CHINA AND MEXICO

★ TRACK IT DOWN ★

**15414 N. 19th Avenue, Suite K
Phoenix, AZ 85023
602-375-3639
www.chinobandido.com**

When I opened Tex Wasabi's Southern Style Barbecue and Sushi, people thought I was crazy. Well, it's awful nice to come down here to Phoenix, Arizona, and find out that there's another group with a screw loose—doing off-the-hook and outta-bounds Chinese and Mexican.

Arizona natives Eve and Frank Collins opened this place eighteen years ago. "Before we opened," Frank says, "she sat up in bed and said, 'What are we going to serve?' And I said, 'Well, the food that we eat at home.'" That meant the Mexican food that's so big in Arizona, the Chinese food Eve grew up with, and the Caribbean food that some friends turned them on to. Like the jerk chicken that Frank says is named after a yet-unknown customer.

You can have a combination of everything on your platter and mix it and match it, like a quesadilla, Cuban black beans, and egg foo young. Or try carnitas next to jade red chicken with jerk

fried rice and Cuban black beans, or a burrito filled with Chinese jenred pork next to Chinese pork fried rice, Jamaican jerk chicken, and refried beans.

They could make 96,420 different combinations, when you do the math. There's something for everybody.

Eve's red sauce for jade red chicken starts in the wok with sesame oil and red chili oil with something secret mixed in, and then ketchup goes right into the hot oil (never seen that be-

"Guy, you better write nice about us, or I will smack you with this spatula!"

fore, but as Eve says, it forms a glaze), and then the garlic. It's like a ketchup hot tub in Flavortown. Sugar goes in next, then chopped green onions, and it boils down. I am standing there, just in awe. Then she dips cubed chicken thighs in slightly whipped egg whites seasoned with black pepper and a little garlic salt. She covers them in pure cornstarch, shakes them free of the excess, and deep-fries them in oil. The whipped egg whites keep the chicken light and crispy. Then she tosses them in the sauce. That's hot and awesome however you get it—with rice, in a burrito, or in a quesadilla.

Eve says she burned rice until she was twenty, but nothing's burning now, except your mouth, maybe. They do a Mexican shredded beef that gets stir-fried in the wok over high heat. It's dynamite, and so is the pollo diablo. It came originally from a Chinese recipe that uses calamari and shrimp. But Eve first blends up serrano peppers—seeds and all—for the kick, then stirs in garlic, onion and green onion, crushed red pepper flakes, and garlic salt. That sits for a couple of days, then she combines it with the fried chicken, cooked up in the wok. The crunch is phenomenal, and the flavor is massive. What a winner chicken dinner.

Eve and Frank have quite a following—even one fan who made his own T-shirt that says BODY BY CHINOS. Loyal, very loyal. This place is great, probably one of the funkiest places we've shot on *DD&D*.

Pollo Diablo (Garlicky, Spicy, Deep-Fried Chicken)

ADAPTED FROM A RECIPE COURTESY OF EVE COLLINS OF CHINO BANDIDO

Here's an at-home version of this dynamite, spicy chicken fusion.

4 SERVINGS

Garlic Mixture

¼ cup minced garlic

1 teaspoon minced yellow onion

1 tablespoon minced green onion, white and green parts

Pinch of crushed red pepper flakes

½ teaspoon freshly ground black pepper

½ serrano pepper, stemmed, seeded, and minced

½ jalapeño pepper, stemmed, seeded, and minced

Pinch of garlic salt

Pinch of garlic powder

Corn oil, for deep frying

¾ cup egg whites (from about 6 large eggs)

2 boneless, skinless chicken breasts cut into ½-inch pieces (about 12 ounces)

2 boneless, skinless chicken thighs cut into ½-inch pieces (about 12 ounces)

⅛ teaspoon garlic salt

⅛ teaspoon freshly ground black pepper

3 cups cornstarch

2 tablespoons hot chili oil, divided

2 teaspoons toasted sesame oil, divided

⅔ cup freshly chopped green onions, white and green parts

Pinch of garlic salt

1. Combine all the ingredients for the garlic mixture in a small bowl.

2. Heat about 5 inches of oil in a deep, heavy-bottomed pot or a deep-fryer until a deep-fry thermometer reads 375°F. Line a plate with paper towels.

3. In a medium bowl, beat the egg whites with a handheld mixer until frothy. Add the chicken pieces, turning to coat each piece evenly. Season with garlic salt and black pepper and stir to distribute.

4. Put the cornstarch in a shallow bowl. Lift the chicken from the egg whites, letting the excess liquid fall back into the bowl. Dredge the chicken pieces in the cornstarch, turning to coat evenly.

5. When ready to fry, pick up about half the chicken in handfuls and transfer from hand to hand to shake off most of the cornstarch. Carefully add the chicken to the oil. After 10 to 15 seconds, stir, or shake the deep-fry basket, to make sure the pieces aren't sticking together. Fry until the chicken floats to the top of the oil and

I'm the one on the right.

is light brown, 3 to 5 minutes. (The chicken should appear somewhat dry, not oily, when lifted from the oil.) Drain on the paper towels. Repeat with the remaining chicken.

6. Heat a wok or a skillet over medium to high heat and add 1 tablespoon of the hot chili oil and 1 teaspoon of the sesame oil. Add half the garlic mixture and half the green onions and stir-fry, taking care not to let the garlic brown. Add half the fried chicken and toss to coat with the sauce. Season with garlic salt and toss once more. Repeat with the remaining ingredients and chicken. Serve.

Joe's Farm Grill

EST. 2006 ★ A BURGER STAND IN AGRITOPIA

★ TRACK IT DOWN ★

**3000 E. Ray Road
Gilbert, AZ 85296
480-563-4745
www.joesfarmgrill.com**

We heard about this joint where they're cooking what they grow, and I had to check it out. It's a burger joint, but it's so not a burger joint.

Joe Johnston's family has been farming here on this land since the early 1960s. The building the restaurant's in was originally their house, and what used to be a hundred fifty acres is now fifteen, set aside for urban organic farming. They take as much as they can for the restaurant, straight from the fields. What they have to bring in from the outside is mostly local, organic, or natural. Kitchen manager Chad Burnett is the guy putting it all together on the plate. They crank out fourteen hundred a week of their Arizona-farm-raised beef patties, pressed thin to cook quick. They've got toppings that most people wouldn't expect at a burger joint. There's fresh mozzarella, apple-cider-smoked bacon, and pepperoni—but then there's the roasted red peppers, which they grow, and a pesto made from their farm's basil, and right-off-the-farm arugula, which will blow your mind. That's a mac daddy patty.

They do a grilled portobello mushroom burger, a homegrown beet salad, and a seared ahi tuna sandwich with the most amazing Asian slaw. Nothing's typical here. They serve sweet potato fries with pineapple serrano dip, and their onion rings are coated in Japanese-style bread crumbs and fresh herbs: that's capital K crunchy. Those are too legit to quit.

GUY ASIDE

It was a very sad day for me when I landed to go to Joe's. My manager, Jack Levar, one of my best friends in the world, had had a heart attack the week before and had been in a coma. Just as I was pulling up to Joe's, I was on the phone with his daughter, who told me that he was not going to recover. It was such a sad, emotional time, but the energy and the enthusiasm of Joe's Farm Grill was a very nice distraction for a few hours. They've created a very special feel to the place, and they're great people.

And check this out-of-the-box pie: grilled barbecue chicken pizza just like the one I've been doing at Johnny Garlic's for years. After rolling the bakery-made dough out into an oblong, Chad grills it quickly on each side, halfway cooking it. Then he sprinkles on the cheese mix: grated fontina, pecorino romano, fresh mozzarella slices, and crumbled blue cheese. Next comes the chopped grilled chicken, diced red onion and tomatoes, and the crown jewel, the apple-cider-smoked bacon. It's practically a Cobb salad on top of the pizza skin. Joe's real barbecue sauce is drizzled over the top before they place the whole thing on the back of the grill to finish. Sprinkled with some of that super-fresh chopped basil, it made my mouth start watering. I didn't need a knife and fork, just a treadmill. The crust has a nice char, there's a huge cheese flavor, there's the sweet and sour of the onion, the sauce is legitimate, and the basil is so forward. This is a pizza chain killer.

The soda fountain organ at Joe's Farm Grill.

Asian Slaw with Spicy Thai Vinaigrette

ADAPTED FROM A RECIPE COURTESY OF JOE'S FARM GRILL

For best results, get the freshest, off-the-farm herbs and vegetables you can find. People do order it by itself as a side, not just on the ahi, it's that good. The vinaigrette will have a more robust flavor if prepared one day in advance. Whisk again just before adding it to the slaw.

6 SERVINGS AS A SIDE

1 cup finely shredded green cabbage (inner leaves preferred)

3 cups finely shredded red cabbage (inner leaves preferred)

3 cups finely shredded napa cabbage (inner leaves preferred)

½ cup julienned (cut into matchsticks) green onion

¼ cup julienned (cut into matchsticks) red bell pepper

2 cups coarsely shredded carrots

Kosher salt and freshly ground black pepper

About 1 cup Spicy Thai Vinaigrette, or to taste (recipe follows)

1. Combine the vegetables in a large mixing bowl, season with salt and pepper, and toss to combine. Dress the mixture in Spicy Thai Vinaigrette to taste.

Spicy Thai Vinaigrette

⅓ cup rice wine vinegar

2 teaspoons fresh lime juice, or to taste

2 to 3 tablespoons garlic-chili sauce (available in Asian markets)

1½ teaspoons honey

1 teaspoon minced peeled fresh ginger

1 teaspoon minced garlic

1 tablespoon freshly chopped basil leaves

1 tablespoon freshly chopped mint leaves

1 tablespoon freshly chopped cilantro leaves

¼ teaspoon freshly ground black pepper

1½ teaspoons toasted black sesame seeds (available in Asian markets)

½ teaspoon ground coriander

Kosher salt

1 tablespoon toasted sesame oil

½ cup peanut oil

1. Whisk all the ingredients except for the oils in a large mixing bowl. Slowly drizzle in the oils while whisking. Taste and season with more salt and lime juice if needed.

They still have a fireplace in this house-turned-burger-joint.

Thee Pitts Again

EST. 1979, RE-EST. 1995 ★ SERVING UP THE BARBECUE OF CHAMPIONS

Something's a little strange here. Sure looks like a diner, but it's in Glendale, Arizona, oh yeah, and they're serving southern-style barbecue, you know, low and slow. But they tell me this guy is a competitive barbecue champion who's won some of the biggest competitions in the country—with more than three hundred awards under his belt.

> ★ TRACK IT DOWN ★
>
> **5558 W. Bel Road**
> **Glendale, AZ 85308**
> **602-996-7488**
> **www.theepittsagain.com**

And it's those award-winning recipes that Roger Wagner is pulling out for the neighborhood crowd, every day. The brisket, the pulled pork, all the classics are done in his mesquite-fired smoker, and besides those he does a few unique items, like a pork sundae. It's got pulled pork, sauce, and some beans—my kinda dessert. He even smokes shrimp, which he finishes on the grill, and catfish.

The day after the show aired it was like we were a new restaurant on grand opening day. We have doubled our staff and business has increased five times. Your show saved us, and we are so very grateful.

—ROGER, CHERYL, CHRIS, AND
MEGAN WAGNER, THEE PITTS AGAIN

Now, I had to ask, how do you make the all-important rub, O wise one? He takes seasoned salt, Spanish paprika, sugar, granulated garlic, cumin, onion salt, and parsley, then adds his special secret mix-in—he's the only one who makes the rub at Thee Pitts, total lockdown. It's very versatile, proof of which is he's won using it on everything from chicken to ribs. He's even smoking whole turkeys with it.

He first spreads margarine over the turkey, to give it a glaze but also to let the seasoning adhere to it. He smokes a large turkey for about fourteen hours and then serves it pulled. It sure is tender and moist, and it tastes great with Roger's homemade sauce. He starts the sauce with brown

Diner meets BBQ joint—a *DD&D* first.

THEE PITTS AGAIN: THE HISTORY

Back in 1979, Roger became a night cook at a place called Thee Pitts in Phoenix. One day the owner asked him if he would like to compete in a barbecue competition in Scottsdale representing Thee Pitts. Of course, he subsequently won, and the owner then offered him part-ownership in the restaurant. They were open for eight years before closing, when the Wagner family moved to Michigan. They did catering there and Roger worked at a meat- and fish-packing plant in Detroit, educating himself more about cuts of meat. They finally returned to Arizona in 1995 and reopened as a family-run restaurant, calling it Thee Pitts Again in the hope of drawing back old customers. Arizona's happy to have them back.

sugar, then a mixture that's mostly Worcestershire sauce, but also a secret, then he puts in a heap of mustard and Heinz ketchup, and it's good to go—no cooking involved. It goes well with everything, especially the best-selling pulled pork.

Listen to what a few regulars had to say:

"It gets the mouth going."

"He eats it, sleeps it, and dreams it."

"He's a champ in our eyes, as well as the rest of the world's."

Yup, Roger's the real deal.

Roger's Wife Cheryl's Simple Chili

ADAPTED FROM A RECIPE COURTESY OF CHERYL WAGNER OF THEE PITTS AGAIN

It may be radio silence on some of Roger's recipes, but Cheryl could win some awards of her own with this classic, simple chili.

12 SERVINGS

2 tablespoons vegetable oil

1 medium onion, chopped

3 to 4 garlic cloves, sliced

1 pound ground beef

1 pound ground turkey

1 tablespoon seasoned salt

1 tablespoon chili powder

2 (15-ounce) cans tomato sauce

2 (15-ounce) cans stewed tomatoes

2 (15-ounce) cans chili beans

2 cups tomato juice

2 to 3 tablespoons chopped fresh flat-leaf parsley

2 to 3 bay leaves

1. Heat the oil in a large Dutch oven or soup pot over medium-high heat. Add the onion and garlic and cook until lightly browned. Add the ground beef, ground turkey, seasoned salt, and chili powder and cook, stirring, until the meat browns. Add the remaining ingredients and mix well. Adjust the heat so the chili simmers and cook until thick and the flavors come together, at least 2 hours.

2. Remove the bay leaves. Serve.

Cheryl's Coleslaw

ADAPTED FROM A RECIPE COURTESY OF CHERYL WAGNER

Roger's wife, Cheryl, is responsible for all the sides, for which she uses old family recipes, like this one.

MAKES ABOUT 12 CUPS

1 large head of green cabbage, chopped

½ large onion, chopped

½ green or red bell pepper, chopped

1 tablespoon freshly ground black pepper

1 tablespoon salt

1 tablespoon celery seed

¼ cup apple cider vinegar

3 carrots, shredded

1 cup mayonnaise

3 to 4 tablespoons sugar, or to taste

1. Toss the cabbage, onion, and bell pepper together in a large bowl. In another bowl, mix all the other ingredients. Toss the slaw mixture with the dressing. Cover and refrigerate for 2 to 4 hours, or until ready to serve.

Baby Blues Bar-B-Q

EST. 2004 ★ A CROSS-COUNTRY TOUR OF GREAT BBQ

★ TRACK IT DOWN ★

**444 Lincoln Boulevard
Venice, CA 90291
310-396-7675
www.babybluesvenice.com**

Venice, California: you gotta love the weather, the beach, the characters, the food. But I gotta be honest with you; when I was here I wasn't thinking about southern-style barbecue—until I found this joint. Wow!

Sure, we do barbecue out here on the West Coast. It's called grilling. But owners Danny Fischer and Rick McCarthy are doing totally off-the-hook, one-of-a-kind Southern California barbecue. Danny says, "People don't understand it, they think we're reinventing the wheel here, they're just not used to it. This seems natural to us. When people ask us what kind of barbecue this is, it's really hybrid barbecue." So dry rub is Texas, vinegar-based is the Carolinas, and then red sauce in general gets that Kansas City spin. These two East Coast transplants pull the best from each and put together a menu that is a virtual tour of great barbecue.

They've got baby back ribs that are tender, tender; Memphis-style ribs that have that deeper, meatier flavor and texture; and Texas beef ribs that are Paul Bunyan–size, all meat. But the real ace up their sleeves is the pulled pork. They start with a dry rub that has about nineteen herbs and spices in it and coat the pork butt, which will sit in the cooler for 24 hours. They then smoke it for 16 to 18 hours, during which time a Guinness is added to the pan, with some water, for flavor. The meat falls off the bone. Out of the smoker with the pan sauce in the bottom, it's kind of like pulled pork meets au jus French dip.

Danny's father had barbecue restaurants when he was growing up, and Rick's family had soul food restaurants. So it comes from the roots, and then they put a California twist on it. Like their killer mac and cheese made from four cheeses, big flavor. And the grilled corn with chipotle-poblano butter and cotijo cheese sprinkled on top is unreal. But their house-made sauces really set them apart. Their Triple XXX is mixed in special separate buckets because you can never clean out the heat, no matter how hard you try. They put in chopped garlic, pineapple, chipotle pepper, and roasted and pureed Scotch bonnet, poblano, and serrano chiles. Then there's a secret magic syrup that goes in, and finally a cayenne-based pepper sauce is added. They mix it old school. From bucket to bucket, it's like a bucket brigade. They slosh this stuff back and forth, and I said, "You guys are killing me," and offered to buy them a bigger bucket! Once the sauce sits for at least a day, they strain it. And trust me, it would be good on anything.

Home of dueling buckets.

Sautéed Okra

ADAPTED FROM A RECIPE COURTESY OF DANNY FISCHER AND RICK MCCARTHY OF BABY BLUES BAR-B-Q

Here's a little of that soul food they're famous for.

2 TO 4 SERVINGS

2 tablespoons extra-virgin olive oil
1 (10-ounce) package frozen cut okra
2 to 3 garlic cloves, chopped
Salt and freshly ground black pepper
1 (15-ounce) can stewed tomatoes, chopped
Splash of red wine vinegar

1. Heat the olive oil in a medium pan over high heat until just smoking. Break up the frozen okra and add to the pan (take care; it may spatter and flare up). Add all but a pinch of the garlic and season with salt and pepper. Cook, stirring occasionally, until the okra heats up and begins to soften. Then add the tomatoes and cook for 1 minute more. Add a splash of red wine vinegar and the remaining pinch of garlic and cook for 1 to 2 minutes to bring the mixture together. Serve.

3D @ 3B. Right on!

Duarte's Tavern

EST. 1894 ★ HOME OF THE FOOD COMA

Cruising the coast of northern California, you've got to love it: the ocean, the seafood, the farms. And there's this cool place in a little town called Pescadero where the Duarte family has been serving up righteous food for more than four generations.

★ TRACK IT DOWN ★

**202 Stage Road
Pescadero, CA 94060
650-879-0464
www.duartestavern.com**

Tim Duarte says, "One of the ideals of the restaurant, way back when, was to feature local products." (I tell you, what's old is new again.) The bar opened in 1894, then it expanded with the restaurant in 1934. For Tim, everything has to be at least as good as it's always been, so he stays true to the old family recipes, like crab cioppino. It's kind of a tomato-based seafood stew filled with fresh Dungeness crab. In my opinion, there's nothing better than the Dungeness crab. They're so close to Half Moon Bay that they get the crab right off the boat—so they spend a lot of time cracking crab. I refused a bib. I am a machine with this stuff. I slurped so much of it. I don't say this often, but it's some of the best I've had in my life—and I needed a hose after eating it.

And this is one of the few places you can still get a California specialty done right: a big, rich West Coast shellfish called abalone on homemade sourdough. They give two cutlets an egg wash and a light dusting of cracker meal, and then it's onto the flat-top grill. When the cutlets start to get golden brown on each side, they're done and placed onto the bread, served with a slice of lemon. It is *so* pure. It's the bomb, so rich, with deep flavor. It deserves to be eaten in silence.

Now, this is artichoke country, so they've got what's fresh from the Pacific, as well as what's fresh from their own little farm just down the street. They make artichoke soup. Sigh. It starts with butter, chicken broth, and chicken bouillon for intensity, and then the handfuls of artichoke hearts go in. They've been precooked with salt, pepper, oil, and a little garlic—still firm, not overcooked—and then they're pureed, leaving a little texture in there. Tim then adds salt, pepper, and garlic and simmers the soup. At the very end the whipping cream is added. It's been the same recipe since the 1950s. It's nice and velvety and totally worthy of its signature-item status. Tim has people who come in asking, "Is this the place with the artichoke soup?"

Then there's the local California olallieberries pie for dessert. It tastes like blackberries but sweeter. After a slice of that pie it was time for a nice long nap.

Duarte's Crab Cioppino

ADAPTED FROM A RECIPE COURTESY OF DUARTE'S TAVERN

Create this local legend in your kitchen, trust me.

4 SERVINGS

4 tablespoons olive oil

2 medium yellow onions, finely chopped

6 celery stalks, finely chopped

¼ cup finely chopped fresh flat-leaf parsley

3 garlic cloves, finely chopped

1½ teaspoons kosher salt

1 bay leaf

1½ teaspoons dried oregano

1½ teaspoons Italian seasoning

1 teaspoon dried thyme

¾ teaspoon ground cumin

¼ teaspoon crushed red pepper flakes

2 (14.5-ounce) cans diced tomatoes, undrained

1 (15-ounce) can tomato sauce

2½ pounds fresh Dungeness crab, cooked and quartered (your fishmonger can do this for you, or see the Cook's Note on the next page)

12 cherrystone clams, cleaned

12 jumbo white prawns, shell on

1 cup clam juice

½ cup dry white wine

8 ounces fresh cod, cut into 2-ounce pieces

1. Heat the olive oil in a large skillet over medium heat. Add the onions, celery, and parsley and cook, stirring frequently, until the onions are translucent. Add the garlic, salt, and remaining herbs and spices and cook, stirring, until fragrant, about 1 minute. Add the diced tomatoes and tomato sauce. Bring the mixture to a boil, reduce the heat to low, and simmer, uncovered, for 30 minutes, stirring occasionally. The mixture will be very thick. Season to taste and remove the bay leaf.

2. Put half the sauce in a large heavy pot or Dutch oven. Place the crab on top, then the clams, then the prawns. Pour in the clam juice, wine, and remaining sauce and top with the cod. Cover the pot and bring the cioppino to a boil over medium-high heat. Immediately turn the heat to medium. When the fish is cooked and the clams are open (the timing will vary depending on the size of the clams—large clams can take as long as 15 minutes to open; discard the closed ones), the cioppino is ready. Serve immediately with a good crusty sourdough bread.

COOK'S NOTE: To cook Dungeness crabs, steam live crabs for 15 minutes over boiling water; crack the shell and remove the head and gills. At the restaurant they crack it at every joint but keep the leg intact so the diners don't end up with lots of tiny pieces.

The seafood gem of the Pacific Northwest, Mr. Dungeness Crab.

El Indio Mexican Restaurant

EST. 1940 ★ HOME OF THE TAQUITO

I love Mexican food. I mean I really love Mexican food. You've got to try this place out in San Diego that makes their own tortillas, hand rolls their taquitos, and is a third-generation family restaurant that's had a loyal following for more than sixty-eight years.

★ TRACK IT DOWN ★

3695 India Street
San Diego, CA 92103
619-299-0333
www.el-indio.com

Any time, morning or night, folks flock here for righteous tamales, chiles rellenos, enchiladas, and plenty more. It was all started back in 1940 by Ralph Pesqueira's father, Ralph Sr., who learned his cooking from his Mexican-born parents. Originally the recipes came from Ralph's grandmother. Everything has homemade seasonings, like the seasoned shredded beef, which I could eat a whole container of, or the shredded chicken cooked with sauce and peppers. Where has *that* been all my life?

The trunk is loaded with tortillas.

Even the beans and salsa are made fresh—and the guacamole, of course, made simply with lime, salt, pepper, tomato, and cilantro. That's good, and so are the fresh corn tortillas, which is how the whole deal got started in the first place. As Ralph tells the tale, "My dad decided he wanted to open up a tortilla shop. He had never made tortillas at home. My grandmother had. So he started making tortillas by hand, and then a group of his friends decided that they would make a tortilla machine. So a machine was built." It was the first one in San Diego. Today's machine is bigger and faster, but they've still got to start by hand. They begin with dried corn kernels, which they heat in hot water to soften up the hard shells. They place them in a machine with a big lava rock wheel in it to grind them up. Let me tell you, even fresh out of the machine, that masa's got some real flavor. Then they drop it into the pressing machine, where it's pressed into 6¾-inch tortillas and cooked. You grab them off the conveyor belt and stack them in piles of twelve. Umm, remember that episode of Lucille Ball? That was me. It sounds easier than it is. They're awesome, and when you're standing in line to order, they'll throw you one.

I just can't keep up, Ralph—it's too fast.

Taquito 101.

Meanwhile, the tortillas get stuffed with beef, chicken, or fish, covered in a red chile sauce to make cheese enchiladas, and cut up and fried to make home-made chips. Or they're rolled and fried to make one of my favorites, taquitos. Man, they're good. And they should be: Ralph's father started making them during World War II when the Consolidated factory across the street from his tortilla factory began requesting lunch items.

And check out the handmade chiles rellenos. They start with a California green chili pepper wrapped around a mild Cheddar cheese on a stick, and it goes into an egg-flour batter, then it's fried. The peppers are money. They also do tamales with their fresh-ground corn masa, stuffed with beef and the traditional olive in the middle, wrapped tightly in a corn husk and steamed. You remove the husk, pile on the toppings, and enjoy.

So swing on by. Ralph and his daughter Jennifer are continuing the tradition, one awesome taquito at a time.

Beef Taquitos

ADAPTED FROM A RECIPE COURTESY OF EL INDIO MEXICAN RESTAURANT

And here it is, the mother (or rather father) of all taquito recipes, straight from the source.

MAKES 24 TAQUITOS

2 (12-ounce) cans roast beef with gravy, or about 3 cups shredded cooked pot roast

Water or beef broth

1 tablespoon kosher salt

1 teaspoon garlic powder

½ teaspoon paprika

1 cup prepared tomato salsa

24 (6-inch) corn tortillas

Vegetable oil, for frying

8 ounces shredded Mexican mixed cheese

1 cup shredded iceberg lettuce

Special equipment: **24 toothpicks**

1. If using the canned meat, put it in a colander and rinse off the gravy. Put the beef into a saucepan with just enough water or broth to cover. Heat until the liquid boils. Remove the beef from the liquid, reserving the broth. Shred the meat, if necessary, and season with salt, garlic powder, and paprika.

2. Add about ¼ cup of the salsa (or as much as you like) to 1 cup of the reserved beef liquid and mix into the shredded meat to add moisture and flavor.

3. To make the taquitos: Wrap 3 or 4 of the tortillas at a time in a tea towel and heat them in the microwave until soft and pliable, about 20 seconds. (Alternatively, put the wrapped tortillas in a tortilla warmer and heat in a 350°F oven.) Take care not to overheat the tortillas or they'll get tough. Repeat with the remaining tortillas.

4. Mound about 2 tablespoons of the meat across the center of a tortilla, leaving a border about ¾ inch from the outside edges of the tortilla. Fold the edge of the tortilla closest to you over the filling, tuck it tightly over the filling, and then roll the tortilla away from you to form a tight roll. Secure the taquito with a toothpick. Repeat with the remaining tortillas and filling. (Practice will always make you a better taquito maker.)

5. To fry the taquitos: Heat a couple inches of oil in a deep, heavy-bottomed pot until a deep-fry thermometer reads 350°F. Line a plate with paper towels. Fry 3 to 4 taquitos at a time until crisp-tender—about the texture of a regular potato chip. (You don't want the taquitos to be hard.) Drain on paper towels and remove the toothpicks.

6. Serve the taquitos warm with salsa, cheese, and lettuce on top.

Aaahhh . . . that is hot!

Emma Jean's Holland Burger Café

EST. 1947 ★ THE CLASSIC TRUCK STOP OFF ROUTE 66

Here on the California side of Route 66, just outside Victorville, it's so hot, there are tons of trucks, and it's time to play the "Where am I going to stop and eat?" game. With my keen powers of observation I suss out the spot where the truckers eat: Emma Jean's Holland Burger Café. Folks around here say it's a trucker's paradise.

★ TRACK IT DOWN ★

**17143 D Street on Route 66
Victorville, CA 92394
760-243-9938**

After sixty years on this stretch of Route 66, Emma Jean's is just like it was. It's still the must stop for great home cooking. For Brian Gentry and his wife, Shawna, keeping it like it was is the way it is.

"We bought the place when I was thirteen," says Brian. Dad was a truck driver, mom was a waitress. Brian's dad was driving Route 66 hauling cement for thirty-one years, and had been coming in here since it had opened. His mother eventually worked here, and they bought the place in 1979. It's always been the Holland Burger, since 1947, but his mom added her name, Emma Jean. Now Brian's raising the third generation in here, with his little daughter, Sarah, at his side. When people come in they step back into a time before chain res-

GUY ASIDE

This is the quintessential example of pulling off the main road, jumping on that stretch of Route 66, and coming across a place with no glitz or glamour to it. You'd probably blow right by; but they've got some great family history and stories inside. And the biscuits—the guy was a biscuit-making machine. Next time you're going through a small town, stop and check out places like this.

Emma Jean's or "Big Brian's Biscuit Barn".

taurants ruled the road, when nobody paid with plastic, and when fueling up meant real-deal comfort food.

They've got some signature biscuits with sausage gravy, which Brian learned to make from his mom at the very table he mixes them up on today. He spoons up the ingredients with something that looks like a gravy boat spoon, also from his mom, and mixes the dough as little as possible. "Well, you've got to be nice to your biscuits," insists Brian—clearly channeling Emma Jean. While the biscuits bake up he browns the sausage for the gravy, then adds flour, salt, and pepper and whisks in milk. When the whisk stands up, it's ready. Split the biscuits, spoon the gravy, and I could eat six, maybe twelve of these.

Brian knows it's the stick-to-your-ribs stuff that his crowd's looking for, so he scratch-cooks just about everything. The burgers are huge—like half-pounders—and I bet they're putting fast-food chains out of business for fifty miles in each direction. They keep it simple; it's just a big all-American burger.

The Brian burger was named after Brian himself and features a mildly spicy roasted green chile and a little Swiss-American cheese on Parmesan toast. And the trucker's sandwich is made from fresh-roasted tri-tip. Talk about homemade.

No foie gras, no sushi here, just plain good cookin'—and Brian and Shawna promise that if you come back next week or next year, it'll still be the same.

Trucker Special Sandwich with Roasted Tri-Tip

ADAPTED FROM A RECIPE COURTESY OF BRIAN GENTRY OF EMMA JEAN'S HOLLAND BURGER CAFÉ

Brian cuts these into thirds and serves each piece skewered with a toothpick and a side of macaroni salad. As he says, "Is that Americana, or what?"

Tri-tip is a triangular muscle from the end of the sirloin. It's usually sold whole. To keep it tender, don't cook it past medium, and make sure to slice it across the grain.

4 SERVINGS

Roasted Tri-Tip

2½ pounds tri-tip steak

1 carrot, peeled and sliced

1 celery stalk, chopped

1 onion, diced

3 garlic cloves, smashed

Pinch of dried oregano

Salt and freshly ground black pepper

Sandwiches

2 tablespoons unsalted butter, at room temperature

8 (½-inch-thick) slices sourdough bread

4 slices Swiss cheese

2 whole roasted canned green chiles (Anaheims), split in two

4 slices cooked bacon

1. To prepare the tri-tip: Preheat the oven to 350°F.

2. Set the tri-tip in a roasting pan and scatter the carrot, celery, and onion around the meat. Sprinkle the garlic, oregano, and salt and pepper to taste over all. Add ½ cup water and cover the pan with aluminum foil. Roast for 45 minutes, then uncover and cook for 10 to 15 minutes longer, until the meat is browned or until an instant-read thermometer inserted into the steak reads about 140°F for medium. Transfer the tri-tip to a cutting board and let rest for 10 to 15 minutes. Slice the meat into ¼-inch-thide slices. (Reserve the cooking liquid for soups and gravies.)

3. To build the sandwiches: Spread the butter on one side of each slice of bread. Heat a large skillet over medium heat, and set 4 slices of bread, butter side down, in the skillet. Top each piece of bread with a slice of Swiss cheese. Place sliced meat on top of the cheese, then green chiles, and bacon. Cover with the remaining bread, buttered side up. Brown the sandwiches, turning as needed, until the bread is golden and the cheese melts. You can put a cover on top to make sure it all heats and melts, just at the end.

4. Cut the sandwiches and serve hot.

The cameraman's last picture before he was taken out.

The Original Falafel's Drive-In

EST. 1966 ★ A MIDDLE EASTERN DRIVE-IN

I've tasted my way across the country, and one of the things that I've learned is to expect the unexpected. I'd expect to find great food in San Jose, California, but what's unexpected is that it would be a fried falafel from a drive-in.

★ TRACK IT DOWN ★

**2301 Stevens Creek Boulevard
San Jose, CA 95128
408-294-7886
www.falafelsdrivein.com**

Falafel are made of deep-fried chickpeas, and they've been fast food in the Middle East forever. As the owners say, "Feeling awful, have a falafel." And people do; the place is always crowded. Joanne Boyle, a daughter of owner Zahie Nijmeh, proclaims, "It's my father's recipe, and it will never change. No one can touch it, it's amazing." Her father was Anton Nijmeh; he had a passion for food and was always in the kitchen. After immigrating here with his family, he bought the place in 1966 and, noting that everybody served burgers, thought he'd bring something from home to the area. No one knew what a falafel was back then, and he made them try it—transitioning the local palates by serving burgers, too. Today, Joanne works the window while the Nijmehs' son-in-law Nassif Grayeb works the line. He's the *falafelator*, he makes them so fast.

They soak the chickpeas overnight, then grind them in something huge that looks like Snuffleupagus. (It's big enough to get rid of a body, but don't hold on to that image.) Then they season the chickpeas with spices, add parsley, and continue to mix. Next step is to form them into falafel balls and line them up in a single layer in the fryer basket. Nassif says to put them into the hot oil real slow, otherwise they'll just break apart. You hold them just-covered with oil for about thirty seconds, then you lower them completely and let them sit for three and a half or four minutes, until deep golden brown. You can eat them straight up—that's some awesome falafel. Or you can have them in a salad or in a pita sandwich with some lettuce, tomato, and homemade tahini—that's a sesame sauce—and a killer hot sauce. It's fantastic: the kitchen uses soybean oil, and it fries so hot that the falafel are not oily. They're *falafelicious*. I'm changing their name to Falafel King.

They get truckers, suits, and kids coming from far and wide for this stuff, but they've also got a whole menu of Middle Eastern delights like gyro, baba ghanoush, and a spiced beef kabob that makes like their version of a burger in a pita.

Another house specialty is their banana shake. Joanne explains that Anton loved fresh fruit, and bananas were the only type he could get year-round at the time, so he mixed them up. The taste? That's literally bananas. It puts out the fire of the hot sauce, so falafel and a banana shake is the hot combo special on the menu.

This many years later, a lot of the regulars still don't know what a falafel is; they just say, "It's made yummily." That works.

They shoulda called it Falafel's Wait-In . . . *Line*. It's that busy and that good.

Falafel

ADAPTED FROM A RECIPE COURTESY OF NASSIF GRAYEB OF THE ORIGINAL FALAFEL'S DRIVE-IN

Remember to fry in soybean oil, as Nassif does, for best results. And remember to soak the chickpeas the night before you want to make these.

MAKES 40 SMALL FALAFEL

1 cup dried chickpeas

1 large onion, finely chopped

3 tablespoons chopped fresh cilantro leaves

1 teaspoon ground coriander

1 teaspoon ground cumin

2 tablespoons all-purpose flour

Kosher salt and freshly ground black pepper

Soybean oil, for deep-frying

Serving suggestions: **pita breads, shredded lettuce, diced tomatoes, diced cucumbers, tahini, and hot sauce**

1. Put the chickpeas in a bowl and cover generously with cold water. Cover and set aside at room temperature to soak overnight.

2. The next day, drain the chickpeas. Finely grind the chickpeas in a food processor. Transfer the ground chickpeas to a large bowl and mix in the onion, cilantro, coriander, cumin, and flour. Season with salt and pepper to taste.

3. Heat a couple of inches of oil in a heavy-bottomed pot or deep-fryer until a thermometer reads 350°F. Line a plate with paper towels. Fry the falafel in batches until crispy. Drain on the paper towels. Serve the balls tucked into pita breads with lettuce, tomatoes, cucumbers, tahini, and hot sauce.

Tabbouleh

ADAPTED FROM A RECIPE COURTESY OF NASSIF GRAYEB

This is a classic Middle Eastern side that goes great with Falafel's falafel.

8 SERVINGS

1 cup fine cracked bulgur wheat

1 cup minced fresh flat-leaf parsley leaves

½ cup minced fresh mint leaves

2 cucumbers, peeled, seeded, and diced

3 tomatoes, diced

½ cup finely chopped yellow onion

3 tablespoons extra-virgin olive oil

3 tablespoons lemon juice, or to taste

1 teaspoon sea salt, plus more to taste

Freshly ground black pepper

1. Put the bulgur wheat in a large bowl. Pour 1 cup water over the wheat. Cover and let stand until the wheat is tender and the water is absorbed, about 20 minutes.

2. Add the herbs, cucumbers, tomatoes, and onion and toss with the mix.

3. Whisk the oil, lemon juice, and 1 teaspoon salt in a small bowl. Pour the dressing over the salad and mix well. Season with salt and pepper to taste. Refrigerate until ready to serve.

Hodad's

EST. 1969 ★ NO SHIRT, NO SHOES, NO PROBLEM

★ TRACK IT DOWN ★

**5010 Newport Avenue
Ocean Beach, CA 92107
619-224-4623**

Ocean Beach, California, is home to great surf, a lot of really cool, laid-back people, and a little place called Hodad's, which is in my opinion what a local burger joint oughtta be: No Shirt, No Shoes, No Problem. Just like the sign says.

According to owner Mike Hardin, a hodad is a surfer term from the early 1960s. It's someone who hangs out on the beach, and they've got a nice board and you always see them around, but they don't know how to surf. When Mike wasn't surfing, he grew up at Hodad's. His parents starting running it in '73, and he took over in '84 and gave the place his own sense of style. Laid-back surfer attitude aside, this guy's cranking out some bodacious beachside burgers.

"No fancy frills, just old-fashioned, sloppy, run-down-your-arm hamburgers," insists Mike. He's got a tattoo of a hamburger on the back on his leg that is just a tiny bit smaller than the double. That's a big tat. Each burger starts with fresh ground beef, never frozen. That makes a difference, says Mike. He makes them on the flat top, and the patty is bigger than the bun. He's known for his outta-bounds bacon cheeseburgers, made his own unique way. See, he wants the burgers to be big, and he doesn't want two little strips of bacon. He wants to make a bacon

patty. So he boils several strips of bacon in water, strains it out, puts it on the grill, flattens it out, turns it over—Mike points out it looks almost like hash browns at this point. The bacon patty should be as big as the burger, or even bigger, when you're done. You slap it on top of the beef, then put down two slices of cheese. Then the whole thing gets put together in a very specific way. He takes the bottom bun, spreads on more mayonnaise than mustard, then

Ocean to yer left, one block.

builds a little "onion castle" of raw rings in a pile on top of that. Then the ketchup is squirted on top of the onions, then slices of pickles, two thick slices of tomatoes, and then the "lettuce snowball" of shredded lettuce goes on top of that. Now, you're ready for the bacon cheeseburger patty and top bun. How do you get your mouth around it? Mike wraps it all in paper—like a little paper diaper, but so you can see everything, "'Cause ninety percent of your tastebuds are in your eyeballs." Don't be intimidated: on Wednesdays Mike offers lessons on how to eat it. He says he can get you down to two napkins. Yeah . . . right.

You've got to lean over. "Trough it," says Mike. He could tell I'd been eating my whole life, and I didn't ruin my wardrobe for the rest of the day.

Mike plays this game in his head that everyone who comes in is a world-renowned food critic. Let's just say, he makes sure the burgers come out right, and so do the tuna salads and the BLTs. And his seventeen-year-old son, Shane, is making the real-deal milkshakes. Was he bred to make milkshakes? "Actually, he was born with a greasy spoon in his mouth," Mike reveals. Shane uses quality ice cream, milk, malted, and a serious mixer. It all comes in a classic metal shake cup with a huge scoop of ice cream hanging off the side—making Dad proud.

According to Mike, he never took an interior design class in his life—hard to believe with the incredible, colorful collection of vanity license plates plastering every the wall of the place. He's got LIVER and ONIONS, both from Nebraska, VA WOLF and YAHOOO from California, BLUEBYU from Arizona, just to name a few choice ones. The ambience is free and the burgers are insane. And Mike says in his next life, he's coming back as himself. He's having too good a time.

Hodad's Bacon Cheeseburger

ADAPTED FROM A RECIPE COURTESY OF HODAD'S

Fasten your seat belt and roll up your sleeves.

MAKES 4 BURGERS

Hodad's Bacon

1¼ pounds lean bacon ends or thick-cut bacon (available at specialty butchers)

8 slices American cheese

1⅓ pounds fresh ground beef chuck

Kosher salt and freshly ground black pepper

4 (5-inch) hamburger buns

2 tablespoons mayonnaise

2 tablespoons yellow mustard

8 onion slices, about ¼ inch thick

Ketchup

8 dill pickle slices

8 tomato slices, about ¼ inch thick

1 cup shredded lettuce

1. To make Hodad's bacon: Roughly chop the bacon. Put in a saucepan with water to cover. Bring to a boil, reduce to a simmer, cover, and cook until the bacon shreds easily, about 45 minutes. Drain. Chop the bacon fine and portion into 4 patties.

2. Put the bacon patties on a hot griddle (or in a hot skillet) and cover with a griddle weight (or press repeatedly with a spatula). Cook until crisp. Flip over and cook until the second side is crisp as well. Remove the weight and place 2 slices of American cheese on each bacon patty.

3. To make the burgers: Season the beef with salt and pepper and form into 4 patties. Heat a griddle or a large skillet. Cook the burgers to the desired degree of doneness.

4. Toast the buns, opened and cut side down, on the griddle. Slather 2 teaspoons mayonnaise on each of the bottom buns. Then smear 2 teaspoons mustard on top. Grab 2 onion slices and build an onion tower on each bun. Top the onions with a squirt of ketchup (this takes their harshness away). Place 2 pickle slices on the top of the tower. Next, put 2 tomato slices, then top the bottom bun off with a handful of shredded lettuce.

5. Place the cheese-topped bacon patties on the burgers and cover each with a bun. Set the whole thing on top of the prepped bottom buns. Wrap those suckers in a piece of paper and get to eating!

The German rock band the Hamburgers . . . performing nightly.

Ramona Café

EST. 1930S, RE-EST. 1980S ★ WHERE TO FIND THE KING KONG OF CRUST

Ramona, California, is about an hour northeast of San Diego, right at the gateway to the desert. In the middle of town is this little joint owned by the daughter of a local egg farmer. It's the kind of place you'd expect to serve basic café cooking, not a homemade chicken cordon bleu with fresh hollandaise.

★ TRACK IT DOWN ★

628 Main Street
Ramona, CA 92605
760-789-8656
www.ramonacafe.com

And get this, it's deep-fried. I've never seen this dish deep-fried, but owner Sonja Vanderveen explains that it just tastes better with a crispy texture. So do the fried chicken, the chicken-fried steak, and the fish and chips. Even the kid-friendly chicken strips are homemade.

The first stoplight was put in this town in 1979, the year Sonja graduated from high school. She left town for a while to earn a degree in food and nutrition, then came back home, eventually buying the café with the help of her parents and some recipes from her Swiss-born mom. Now I get it: her mother cooked chicken cordon bleu for her when she was a kid, and this was Sonja's natural adaptation.

She pounds out a chicken breast after cutting it in half, places ham and Gruyère cheese in the middle, rolls it up, and secures it with toothpicks. (I'd eat it like that if I liked chicken sushi.) She bakes it, then dips it in eggs, breads it, dips again, and breads again. Then she fries it. She really is the colossal King Kong of Crust. Served with the hollandaise on top, the cheese

I drove a riding lawnmower down this sidewalk for the opening of this episode.

really pops, and the crust on the chicken is soooo crunchy. When she first put it on the menu, people went bananas. Bananas is good.

The key to the crunch is her homemade breading, made from dried-out biscuits, flour, pepper, cayenne, poultry seasoning, and salt. She uses the same breading on her buttermilk fried chicken and her chicken-fried steak— which has a twist. It's a mixture of half ground beef and half ground veal. The breading is not too thick, it's super moist, and you really taste the meat.

Ramona's is just as big for breakfast, with a cheese-topped skillet mix called the Kitchen Sink; the Hawaiian short stack with pineapple, coconut, and whipped cream; and strawberry cream cheese–stuffed French toast. But for a lot of folks, the fresh daily football-size cinnamon rolls are the big draw. It's her mom's recipe; and my son Hunter would go out of his mind for one of these sugary, doughy packets of goodness. You need a rubber spatula to get it off the roof of your mouth. Give one a try: they won first place at the Del Mar Fair.

Everybody is playing hide-and-seek.

Blue-Ribbon Cinnamon Rolls

ADAPTED FROM A RECIPE COURTESY OF SONJA VANDERVEEN OF RAMONA CAFÉ

As Sonja says, be sure to let the "goo" (that's the dough) get "happy" (rise) for an hour before rolling it out.

MAKES 12 ROLLS

Dough

4 large eggs

¾ cup plus 1 tablespoon granulated sugar (6 ounces)

1 teaspoon fine salt

2 cups lukewarm milk

½ cup (4 ounces) margarine, at room temperature

8 cups all-purpose flour, divided

2 tablespoons active dry yeast

Oil, for brushing

Filling

½ cup (4 ounces) margarine, at room temperature

2 cups brown sugar

3 tablespoons ground cinnamon

1 cup pecans, chopped

Glaze

4 cups confectioners' sugar

Pinch of salt

1 tablespoon almond extract

½ cup (4 ounces) margarine, at room temperature

⅓ cup milk

1. For the dough: In a standing mixer fitted with the paddle attachment, beat the eggs, granulated sugar, and salt. Combine the warm milk and margarine and add to the egg mixture. While mixing slowly, gradually add 4 cups of the flour; beat to combine. Add the yeast and mix thoroughly. Add the remaining 4 cups flour and mix on medium speed for about 7 minutes to make a soft dough.

2. Turn the dough out of the bowl. Knead briefly and form into a ball. Put the dough in a lightly oiled bowl. Cover with plastic wrap and set aside at room temperature until doubled in size, about 1 hour.

3. Preheat the oven to 350°F.

4. For the filling: Turn the dough onto a work surface and roll into a 1½ by 2-foot rectangle. Spread the margarine over the dough and sprinkle the entire surface with the brown sugar, cinnamon, and chopped pecans. Roll the dough up into a cylinder starting with a long edge, and then cut into 12 slices. Lay the slices in an oiled baking pan and bake until golden brown, about 15 minutes. Let cool.

5. For the icing: Whisk the confectioners' sugar, salt, and almond extract together in a large bowl. Whisk in a tablespoon of margarine at a time until combined. (This will look a little crumbly.) Slowly whisk in the milk to make a thick glaze. Drizzle the glaze over the rolls; set aside for a couple minutes for the glaze to set. Serve.

Behind her big smile is a cinnamon roll wizard.

Squeeze Inn

EST. 1977 ★ HOME OF THE CHEESE-SKIRTED SQUEEZE BURGER

Nestled between the Sierras and San Francisco, Sacramento has its share of slammin' food. We've found a tiny dive here that is famous for a burger that takes about five napkins to eat: messy, juicy, and tasty. It's the Squeeze with Cheese, an off-the-hook burger covered in Cheddar.

★ TRACK IT DOWN ★

**7918 Fruitridge Road
Sacramento, CA 95820
916-386-8599**

They put as much cheese on this burger as they do meat. What's cool is that they steam the burger with ice, which steams the bun and keeps the burger juicy. The aim is to get a bubbling apron of fried cheese—or a browned "cheese skirt," as they call it—on your burger. So how do you tackle this puppy? The locals have several methods. Some take the skirt off and eat some of it first, to tantalize their taste buds before biting into the juicy burger. Others fold some of the cheese in, and still others recommend holding the burger with one hand, never letting it go, and eating your fries with the other hand. It can get messy.

We all had to *squeeze in* for this photo . . . ha ha ha.

Owner Travis Hausauer bought the place seven years ago and is keeping the thirty-one-year tradition alive and well. A former teacher, he'd never been in the restaurant business before, but when an old army buddy told him the Squeeze Inn was up for sale, he took the plunge and soon had mastered the Squeeze technique. Other menu items to try are the tacos made with premium rib-eye roast and smothered in cheese, and the steak teriyaki sandwich on a sourdough roll with a killer homemade sauce.

No, they're not wrinkled eggs. These are cheeseburgers!

This don't-tell-your-doctor-you-came restaurant is a family affair now, with Travis's father, nieces, nephews, daughter Morgan, and daughter-in-law Katie serving and his son Brandon sharing space behind the griddle. The building itself was originally a lobby from an old pancake house in downtown Sacramento, which was eventually moved to its current location.

Come early: they open at ten, and people are already squeezing in at the eleven-stool counter. But don't worry; although the restaurant might as well be a phone booth, it's got a patio that seats fifty.

> People tell me all the time that they have come from as far as Denver, South Carolina, New York, New Orleans, and more, just to eat at the Squeeze Inn. I'll never forget the kindness and down-to-earth attitude of [David Page's] crew.
>
> —TRAVIS HAUSAUER AND
> THE SQUEEZE INN GANG, SQUEEZE INN

⅓-Pound Squeeze Burger

ADAPTED FROM A RECIPE COURTESY OF SQUEEZE INN

Frying these on a hot griddle, the owner takes a ⅓-pound handful of Cheddar to top a ⅓-pound burger patty. The cheese spreads out, ice is placed around it, and the top bun is put in place before the whole thing is covered to let it steam. They use "flat-top" burgers, which I like because you get that nice caramelized crisp on the meat. So when making the patties, don't make them too round; flatten them out. This really works. You're gonna love it.

MAKES 3 BURGERS

1 pound ground beef (80% lean and 20% fat; you can substitute leaner ground beef, but you'll sacrifice taste)

Lawry's Seasoned Salt

About 1 pound shredded mild Cheddar cheese

Ice cubes

3 good sourdough burger buns, but not hard rolls

Long sliced dill pickles

Sliced red and yellow onions

Sliced tomatoes

Lettuce leaves

1. Divide the meat into 3 evenly sized burgers and season with Lawry's Seasoned Salt to taste. Cook the burgers to the desired degree of doneness on a griddle or in a large cast-iron skillet.

2. Top the burgers with a handful of cheese, then top each one with a bun. Let the cheese melt a bit and then add a couple ice cubes to the pan around the cheese. Cover and cook until the cheese melts completely. (The ice melts and adds just the right amount of steam to melt the cheese and keep the meat moist.)

3. While the cheese melts, make up the bottom buns to your liking with pickles, onions, tomatoes, and lettuce. Once the cheese melts into a skirt around the burger and browns on the bottom, place the burgers on the bottom buns, cheese and all. Cool slightly so the cheese sets. Serve.

Steak Tacos

ADAPTED FROM A RECIPE COURTESY OF SQUEEZE INN

Fried up on the griddle, yes, these have their share of cheese, too.

SERVES 2 (2 TACOS EACH)

2 (4-ounce) rib-eye steaks

Kosher salt and freshly ground black pepper

1 tablespoon vegetable oil, plus more for frying

4 (6-inch) white corn tortillas

2 handfuls shredded mild Cheddar cheese

Serving suggestions: **diced tomato, diced red onion, shredded iceberg lettuce, salsa, sour cream, jalapeños, and avocado**

1. Season the steaks with salt and pepper. Heat a medium-large skillet over medium-high heat. Add 1 tablespoon oil and cook the steaks to the desired degree of doneness. (I like this medium-rare.) Set the steaks aside, but hold on to the skillet.

2. In another small skillet heat about 1 inch of oil over medium heat. Using tongs, slide a tortilla into the hot oil, and cook just until soft and pliable, about 30 seconds. Repeat with the other tortillas. Set the pan aside.

3. Thinly slice the steaks. Lay the softened tortillas on a work surface and divide the meat between the tortillas. Top each steak with some cheese. Fold each filled tortilla over into a taco shape.

4. Add a little hot oil to the medium-large skillet. Cook the tacos in batches, turning once, until crisp on both sides and the cheese melts. Serve the tacos with tomatoes, onions, lettuce, salsa, and other toppings as desired.

Taylor's Automatic Refresher

EST. 1949 ★ BURGERS AND SHAKES, NAPA STYLE

★ TRACK IT DOWN ★

**933 Main Street
St. Helena, CA 94574
707-963-3486
www.taylorsrefresher.com**

When I think of retro drive-ins I think of the Midwest and East Coast, but Napa, California? When you're driving through St. Helena in the wine country, a familiar profile will pop up on the landscape, just as it has for almost sixty years. Welcome to Taylor's Refresher. They've got shiny red picnic table seating and a pretty basic delivery system, intercom and all.

Owners Joel and Duncan Gott bought the place in 1999. Duncan had a deli in Calistoga for about ten years, so they knew what they were doing when they took the place over. They're cranking out stuff like the Miss Kentucky chicken sandwich, sweet potato fries, calamari, and get this: ahi burgers. Just what you'd expect at a drive-in, right? Sushi-grade ahi? It's one of their signature dishes, and it's a great piece of meat. I was in it to win it with this one;

This place rocks the wine country.

I don't get enough sushi on this show and I need my sushi fix now and then. They get their fish out of San Francisco, delivered six days a week, so chances are that your fish was caught that morning. It's dipped in soy sauce, grilled to rare, topped with wasabi ginger mayonnaise and Asian slaw, and there you have it. Wouldn't you love to have a bite of that?

The place had always been a burger joint. They kept the fries from the original menu, but made it over wine-country style. The beef they use is hormone free and California raised. They do a western bacon blue ring burger (blue cheese, fried onion ring, and bacon). The blue cheese melts in this cradle of fried (onion) friendship before it's taken off the grill. The Wisconsin burger is grilled mushroom, bacon, Cheddar, and homemade barbecue sauce on sourdough. It's all about the quality.

Duncan's burgers are the real deal, but this place ain't a one-trick pony. They do quarter-pound all-beef hot dogs and 1950s-style milkshakes—of which they sell a couple hundred a day, gaining the sometime nickname "the shake brothers." Yet another signature item they do up right here is the fish and chips. American drive-in meets British favorite—with good batter and good fresh fish. They use grade-A halibut, and the batter's got San Francisco's own Anchor Steam beer in there. The carbonation helps keep the crust light and crispy as it fries. Served with a little tartar sauce, slaw, and some lemon over fries, that's killer.

Their first night the Gott brothers served six or seven hundred people, ran out of food for day two, put up a sign that said WATER MAIN BROKE, got more supplies, and reopened on Sunday. It was classic. And the fun never stopped: they went on to win an American Classic James Beard Award. This is the kinda place that makes standing in line worth the wait, and yes, this is wine country; you can enjoy a nice vintage with your burger, too.

Get this man some shades!

Ahi Burger

ADAPTED FROM A RECIPE COURTESY OF TAYLOR'S AUTOMATIC REFRESHER

There's not one part of this sandwich that I don't love; it's a delicious combination of hot and cold.

4 SERVINGS

Oil, for grilling

4 (4-ounce) sushi-grade ahi tuna steaks, 1 inch thick

Soy sauce, for dipping

4 egg buns or other soft sandwich buns, split open

Ginger-Wasabi Mayonnaise (recipe follows)

Asian Slaw (see page 209)

1. Heat a grill so it's good and hot. Brush the grill lightly with oil. Dip the tuna in the soy sauce and grill until charred on the outside but still raw in the center, 1 to 2 minutes on each side. In the meantime, toast the buns on the grill until hot and crunchy.

2. Set the tuna on the buns and top with Ginger-Wasabi Mayonnaise and some Asian slaw.

Ginger-Wasabi Mayonnaise

MAKES ABOUT 1⅓ CUPS

1 cup mayonnaise

¼ cup pickled ginger, rinsed, drained, and finely chopped

1 to 2 tablespoons wasabi powder (depending upon desired heat)

1½ teaspoons extra-virgin sesame oil

1 tablespoon fresh lime juice

1½ teaspoons soy sauce

1. Whisk all the ingredients together in a bowl. Cover and refrigerate for at least 2 hours or up to 3 days in advance for the flavors to come together. Serve.

Asian Slaw

MAKES ABOUT 3 CUPS

Dressing

3 tablespoons rice wine vinegar

3 tablespoons thinly sliced green onion, white and green parts

1 tablespoons plus 1 teaspoon extra-virgin sesame oil

1 tablespoon sherry vinegar

1 tablespoon soy sauce

1 tablespoon hoisin sauce

1 tablespoon sriracha hot sauce

1 tablespoon honey

1 tablespoon pickled ginger, rinsed, drained, and chopped

½ teaspoon minced peeled fresh ginger

½ tablespoon red wine vinegar

1 teaspoon fresh lime juice

½ teaspoon minced garlic

Slaw

2 cups shredded napa cabbage

½ cup shredded purple cabbage

½ cup grated carrots

1. Whisk all the dressing ingredients together in a large bowl.

2. Mix all the slaw vegetables together in a bowl. Toss with the dressing. This can be stored up to 3 days in the refrigerator.

Four Kegs Sports Pub

EST. 1977 ★ HOME OF THE KILLER STROMBOLI

Every once in a while on *Diners, Drive-Ins and Dives* I get to visit one of my favorite places from my past, like this one. When I was going to UNLV, a Saturday afternoon was about watching the game, having a cold brew, and eating some killer stromboli.

★ TRACK IT DOWN ★

**267 N. Jones Boulevard
Las Vegas, NV 89107**
702-870-0255
www.fourkegs.com

If you've never had one, a stromboli is a stuffed pocket of pizza dough filled with anything from Italian cold cuts to meatballs and marinara sauce or even beef and Cheddar. This place may look like just another Vegas bar, but outsiders are missing out: the 'bolis here are some of the best I've ever had.

The stromboli capital of the universe.

Mario Perkins started working in the kitchen at Four Kegs when it opened, two months after he graduated high school. His family moved to Vegas from Brooklyn, where he'd learned his food from an Italian grandmother. Now he's one of the owners, passing it all on to a dedicated crew, some of whom he used to babysit. Other than the 'boli they've got Sicilian pizza, baby back ribs, Philly cheesesteaks, and killer wings; but the 'boli really is one of the best ever.

He wouldn't give me the recipe, but he gave me 80 percent, telling me, "You went to school, you can figure it out." He adds yeast, sugar, salt, water, and flour to make a double-rise dough. On the weekends he's making the dough three or four times a day, always fresh. He then cuts it, portions it, and puts it in his thirty-year-old stromboli pans. The dough rises once more and he gets down to business. Shredded mozzarella cheese goes down the middle, not touching the ends; marinara sauce is spooned on top of that; then you layer the salami, ham, sausage, and pepperoni. It's folded over and closed by pinching the edges.

Next time you roll to Vegas, cruise over to Jones and Highway 95. Ask for my brutha from another mother, Mario, and tell 'em I sent you. He makes the whole experience even better.

Southern Spicy Wings

ADAPTED FROM A RECIPE COURTESY OF MARIO PERKINS OF FOUR KEGS SPORTS PUB

To me, this is how wings are meant to be.

2 TO 3 APPETIZER SERVINGS

Oil, for frying

1 pound chicken wings, tips removed

2 tablespoons habanero hot sauce (recommended: Tabasco)

2 to 3 tablespoons seasoned salt (recommended: Lawry's)

1. Heat oil in a deep-fryer, or heat about 3 inches of oil in a deep, heavy-bottomed pot until a deep-fry thermometer reads 375°F. Line a plate with paper towels.

2. Fry the chicken wings, in batches if needed, until cooked through and crisp, 8 to 10 minutes depending on the size of the wings. Drain on paper towels. Transfer the hot wings to a bowl and toss with the habanero sauce and seasoned salt to taste. Serve.

Three stromboli bad boys.

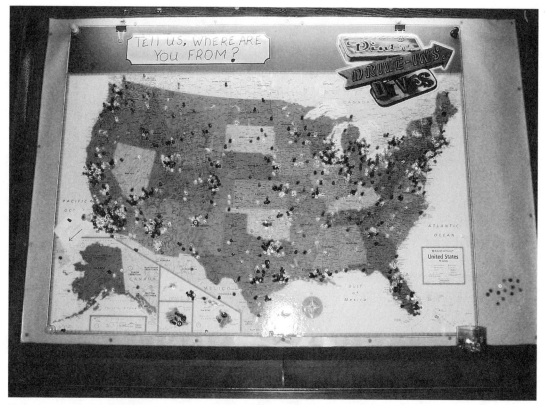

Wow, the great fans of *Triple D,* thanks for recognizing one of my faves.

Monte Carlo Steakhouse

EST. 1972 ★ STEP BACK IN TIME, BEHIND THE BEER COOLER

Here in Albuquerque, if you want a good dinner, hit the liquor store where you'll find a great steakhouse. But you've got to hunt for it. Hint: It's behind the beer cooler.

★ TRACK IT DOWN ★

3916 Central SW
Albuquerque, NM 87105
505-836-9886

Don't be afraid, it doesn't look like a real restaurant until you get inside. The Monte Carlo is an Albuquerque institution: it's the locals' place to come and chill on Route 66. It's a meat and potatoes kind of place. They've got burgers, ribs, steaks, and even a cheesesteak. You don't come here for a tomato and avocado on whole wheat.

The family's been running it for three generations, and they're still all led by Mama. Angelina Katsaros opened the joint with her late husband, Mike. They started making sandwiches, and after a few months someone suggested hamburgers and steaks. They cut rib-eye and sirloin fresh every day, and they're known to be the best in the county. Son Lou Katsaros holds true to his dad's philosophy when it comes to freshness. They slap a rib-eye on a super-hot grill, sprinkle some seasoning salt on top, turn it once for a crosshatch, then flip it and brush it with butter. That is great.

But it isn't just rockin' steaks that get hand-cut here. There's Mama's classic Greek souvlaki, with a family twist. They

Just one of the plates that will rock your palate.

make theirs with pork tenderloin, which they cut into cutlets and marinate with salt, lemon juice, black pepper, white wine, garlic salt, vinegar, and of course oregano—or it wouldn't be Greek. That sits covered in the fridge for five or six days. Then they skewer it and grill it off, basting with olive oil, oregano, salt, pepper, and a little lemon juice. I think I hear the national anthem of Flavortown going off right about now. It's deep, monster flavor; it's like monster-truck pork it's so flavorful.

Mama's Greek recipes just keep on coming: a Greek salad with feta and stuffed grape leaves, fresh-made baklava, and even that Italian classic spaghetti and meatballs with a Greek twist. She says it's the Greek mint that sets them apart. I call it Mama's "money" meatballs.

And then there's Greek chicken. It's a split bird in a pan sprinkled with garlic, oregano, salt, pepper, and olive oil, with butter and some water in the pan. That gets baked off, and it's finger-licking good. It's killer—about as basic as you can make it and about as tender and juicy as you can get it.

I want Mama to mail me food every day. Lou points out, she would, too.

Mike Katsaros, Founder 1928 - 1989

Greek Meatballs (Mama's "Money" Meatballs)

ADAPTED FROM A RECIPE COURTESY OF MONTE CARLO STEAKHOUSE

MAKES ABOUT 24 (2-INCH) MEATBALLS

½ cup olive oil

1 medium onion, finely chopped

1 teaspoon finely chopped garlic

1 teaspoon dried mint

½ teaspoon dried oregano

1 teaspoon kosher salt

2 pounds ground beef

2 large eggs

¾ cup plain dried bread crumbs

1. Heat a large skillet over medium heat and add 3 tablespoons of the olive oil. Add the onion, garlic, mint, oregano, and salt and cook until the onions are tender and the herbs are fragrant, about 6 minutes. Transfer to a large bowl and add the beef, eggs, and bread crumbs. Stir until completely combined. Then, using your hands, form into 2-inch meatballs.

2. Reheat the skillet over medium-high heat with the remaining olive oil. Cook the meatballs in batches as needed until brown on all sides, 4 to 6 minutes. Transfer to a serving platter and serve with marinara sauce and spaghetti.

A darker shirt and hair and I'm in the family.

Louie Mueller Barbecue

EST. 1949 ★ A DOWN-HOME TEXAS PIT

You know it's gotta be good when a downscale place like this draws such an upscale crowd. Some say it's the best barbecue in central Texas. I love barbecue; I own a couple barbecue restaurants in California, Tex Wasabi's; and when I get a chance to try some famous brisket at Louie Mueller's in Taylor, Texas, well, it's a good day.

Bobby Mueller's been running this place for thirty-three years, having taken over from his father, Louie. When he puts the American flag up outside the place, people know it's mealtime. And they line up for legendary brisket, homemade sausage, pork ribs, beef ribs, and anything else Bobby throws in the pit.

At the crack of dawn, he gets his fires going (or "fahrs," as he pronounces it) in the pit, which was built in 1959. But it's not just the pit; everything here is done the old way. Walking in is like going back in time. Your food comes on a butcher-paper-covered tray, and Bobby's right-hand man, Lance Kirkpatrick, keeps the crowds happy with little nibbles. First hit's free.

The brisket's so good people say it doesn't need the sauce. They rub it well with salt and a lot of pepper and then the flavor from the oak fire does the rest. Nothing else, and it's been the same way for more than fifty years. It goes on at four-thirty in the morning and they'll have the last meat on by ten AM.

★ TRACK IT DOWN ★

206 W. Second Street
Taylor, TX 76574
512-352-6206
www.louiemuellerbarbecue.com

GUY ASIDE

This place is one of the most down-home of all barbecues; it speaks nostalgia. The fire pit is so big that if you don't pay attention, you might fall in. I'm standing there talking to the owner and I ask, "Where's the wood come from?" Meaning where'd they buy it. And he drops a piece of wood on the ground and looks at me with the biggest you-dummy look and says, "Trees." I didn't know what to do; I just about died.

They do about forty on a busy day and slice them until they're gone. If you order it "wet," it means you want the back end, which is moist with a little fat on it. And they go through one hundred fifty sausage links at lunch—regular, jalapeño, and chipotle.

Bobby says he retired at sixty-five—a few years ago—but he's still working, and when you watch him you realize he refuses to phone it in, even after all these years. In 2006 they got a James Beard Award. Bobby says it caught him by surprise and that his dad would've been just as flabbergasted. He's a true barbecue icon.

Bobby the Barbecuer.

If the sausage is that big, I want to know who bakes the bun!

Old-Fashioned Potato Salad

ADAPTED FROM A RECIPE COURTESY OF BOBBY MUELLER OF LOUIE MUELLER BARBECUE

What better side than a classic potato salad.

8 TO 10 SERVINGS

3 pounds whole russet potatoes

2 teaspoons kosher salt, plus more for cooking the potatoes

½ cup mayonnaise

⅓ cup dill relish

6 large eggs, hard boiled and diced

3 celery stalks, diced

3 tablespoons prepared mustard, yellow or spicy brown

Freshly ground black pepper

1. Put the potatoes in a large pot of water and season with salt. Bring to a boil and cook until fork tender, about 25 minutes. Drain. Let the potatoes cool, then peel.

2. Dice, crumble, or mash the potatoes into a large bowl. Stir in the mayonnaise, relish, eggs, celery, mustard, 2 teaspoons salt, and pepper to taste. Serve immediately, or refrigerate until serving time.

Mac and Ernie's Roadside Eatery

EST. 1999 ★ THE SHACK OF CULINARY PLEASURES

Here we are in Tarpley, Texas, just about an hour west of San Antonio. They've got about fifty people between signs, as they say, and they've got a post office, a general store, and this funky little joint.

It's a shack, next to a creek, deep in the Texas Hill Country where self-taught chef Naylene Dillingham is cranking out totally rocking food in a tin-roofed open-air kitchen.

★ TRACK IT DOWN ★

**Williams Creek Depot FM 470
Tarpley, TX 78883
830-562-3250
www.macandernies.com**

What do they do when it rains? Speak louder, says Naylene. They're not interested in expanding or changing, as it would change the flavor. And believe me, you don't want to mess with the flavor. She makes New Zealand lamb, country-fried Texas style; local quail in an ancho chile sauce; and tuna in ginger butter. But the dish Naylene started with was the Cabrito Burger. If you don't speak Spanish, *cabrito* means goat. It's 100 percent ground goat—raised by Naylene herself. See, Naylene, her husband, and another couple needed a market for their goats, and this restaurant was the result. She calls them Cabrito Burgers because if you say goat burgers it just doesn't have the same ring. "I wanted to call it a McMutton but you-know-who would serve me if I did that," she explains.

GUY ASIDE

This was one of the first joints we did. Funny thing is it truly is like a shack, a place you might get at Sears to hold your lawn mower—all made out of wood.

I wanted to make one, but she wouldn't tell me what's in it. Hmm . . . I smell garlic, and I can see there's either parsley or cilantro in there. It's eight ounces seared hot, topped with pepper Jack cheese and served with tomato and lettuce on a toasted kaiser roll. It's delicious.

You can enjoy that burger in the parking lot dining room. She calls it a veranda, right behind the general store. After the burgers took off, Naylene started expanding the menu. Now she keeps a small staff busy up front while she's cooking out back—in cramped quarters with all the convenience of a dorm room, crate bookshelves and all.

There's a line that starts at opening. What you get depends on what Naylene feels like cooking the day you show up. There might be salmon, or that local quail with ancho chiles. She takes a dried ancho, removes the seeds, and blends it up with honey and two cloves of garlic. The glaze is brushed on and she crisps up the quail on the grill. The quail look small but they're very rich—and excellent.

Then there's dessert. Some regulars I met call and make a reservation for a piece of pie. You have to lock in on it. One time a guy got the last two chicken-fried lamb chops and the customer behind him offered to buy them from him. Scalping chicken-fried lamb chops? Makes sense to me; I had eight while I was there. Inside this shack, the lady can cook.

Naylene and her husband raise goats. That is a neato . . . cabrito!

Chicken-Fried Lamb Chops with Creamy Gravy

ADAPTED FROM A RECIPE COURTESY OF NAYLENE DILLINGHAM OF MAC AND ERNIE'S ROADSIDE EATERY

The chicken-fried lamb chops were inspired by a friend who missed her daddy's version. It was like a light-bulb that went off in her little head, says Naylene. The gravy is Naylene's mother's recipe. They might be the best lamb chops I've ever had.

6 SERVINGS

Gravy

2 tablespoons olive oil

3 tablespoons all-purpose flour

2 cups whole milk

1 teaspoon kosher salt

1 teaspoon freshly ground black pepper

1 teaspoon turbinado sugar

Lamb

Oil, for frying

2 teaspoons kosher salt

1 tablespoon freshly ground black pepper

2 cups all-purpose flour

12 single-rib frenched lamb chops

2 cups buttermilk

1. For the gravy: Heat the oil in a heavy-bottomed saucepan over medium heat. Sprinkle the flour over the oil and cook, whisking to make a paste (or roux). Cook, whisking constantly, until the mixture turns a light peanut-brown color, about 7 minutes. Whisk in the milk, salt, pepper, and sugar and bring to a boil. Reduce the heat to medium-low or low and simmer, whisking frequently until the sauce thickens enough to coat the back of a spoon (not too thick, but not too thin), about 12 minutes. Keep the gravy warm while you make the chops.

2. For the lamb: Heat about 1 inch of oil in a deep, heavy-bottomed pot until a deep-fry thermometer reads 365°F. Line a plate with paper towels.

3. Mix the salt and pepper with the flour. Dredge the lamb chops in the seasoned flour, then dip them in the buttermilk, and back into the flour. Carefully add 3 to 4 chops at a time to the hot oil and cook, turning once, about 2 minutes per side for medium-rare. Drain on the paper towels.

4. Serve the chops with the gravy.

Maria's Taco Xpress

EST. 1997 ★ FAST FOOD, TEXAS-STYLE

★ TRACK IT DOWN ★

**2529 S. Lamar Boulevard
Austin, TX 78704
512-444-0261
www.tacoxpress.com**

This is a South Austin institution, and it's fast food, Texas-style. There's a lot to love. The locals rave about the fresh corn tortillas, classic Mexican spices, and friendly owner Maria Corbalán, who always calls you "sweetie" when she takes your order.

Maria's an Argentinean immigrant whose only experience in the restaurant biz was waiting tables. She originally bought a very small trailer. She didn't know how to cook, but she learned the old-fashioned way, by making mistakes. Now she's cooking up more than a dozen types of tacos, handmade enchiladas, scratch-made refried beans, and those fresh tortillas. To make her picadillo enchiladas, she first cooks down the ground meat, then throws in some fresh-cut carrots and potatoes, a little garlic powder, cumin, salt, and pepper. Then she adds chipotle pepper, chopped onion, and finally tomato. It all cooks down for fifteen, twenty, twenty-five minutes, whatever Maria's feeling, apparently. For the sauce, she sautés the guajillo peppers on a hot grill, to get a little burn on them, then blends them with a little hot water and strains them to get the skins and seeds out. She puts them back in the blender and adds a little pepper, salt, oregano, garlic, and cumin, adds a little more water, and blends again. She then dips the corn tortilla in the sauce, fries the tortilla on the flat top, adds the picadillo in the middle, and rolls. Plating it up requires a mound of shredded cheese melted on top and a garnish of beans, shredded lettuce, tomatoes, and Mexican rice. The enchilada sauce is dynamite. Great flavor—it's sweet, it's spicy, and frying the tortilla with it on there makes the deal.

Maria makes about two or three thousand tacos here a day. They serve everything from migas tacos with shredded tortilla chips right in the egg to tacos al pastor. I'm an al pastor junkie; it's one of my favorite things. She takes a big cup of guajillo sauce, pineapple, a bit of chopped white onion, cumin, pepper, oregano, garlic, and salt and mixes them in a bowl, then adds it to the cubed pork butt to marinate overnight. The next day she cooks it up on the grill and serves it in tortillas with onion and cilantro. You taste that sweet pineapple right off the bat. Maria says that for real these would be great with chimichurri—so she made me one, and what a treat.

Yep, she'll even top a Mexican classic with an Argentinean hot sauce. What a lady; I see why she's a legend in these parts.

The sign of the times.

Pollo Guisado

ADAPTED FROM A RECIPE COURTESY OF FERNANDO EZETA OF MARIA'S TACO XPRESS

The pollo guisado chicken is a little bit sweet, spicy, tender. It's crazy good.

4 TO 6 SERVINGS

2 pounds boneless, skinless chicken thighs

¾ teaspoon kosher salt, plus more to taste

3 medium tomatoes, diced

¼ cup canned chipotle en adobo sauce

¾ teaspoon ground cumin

¾ teaspoon garlic powder

¾ teaspoon freshly ground black pepper, plus more to taste

3 tablespoons vegetable oil

1 onion, diced

Serving suggestions: **crisp
taco shells, shredded lettuce,
diced tomatoes, and shredded
Cheddar cheese**

The rest of the statue is on layaway.

My Jedi powers just couldn't make it flip off my hand.

1. Put the chicken in a saucepan with salted water to just cover. Bring to a simmer and cook until just cooked through, about 25 minutes. Let cool; shred the chicken.

2. Put the tomatoes, chipotle sauce, cumin, garlic powder, ¾ teaspoon pepper, ¾ teaspoon salt, and 1 cup water in a blender. Puree until smooth.

3. Heat the vegetable oil in a saucepan over medium heat, add the onion, and cook until the onion is golden, about 7 minutes. Add the chipotle mixture and bring to a simmer. Then add the chicken and simmer until the sauce thickens and the chicken is tender, about 15 minutes. Season with salt and pepper to taste.

4. Serve the pollo guisado in crisp tacos shells with lettuce, tomato, and cheese.

DeWese's Tip Top Café

EST. 1938 ★ YOU'LL NEVER LEAVE HUNGRY

. . . .

You know, comfort food may sound simple, but there's a real art to getting it right and keeping it that way—which is what three generations have been doing for seventy years at DeWese's Tip Top Café, here in San Antonio.

> **★ TRACK IT DOWN ★**
> . . . .
> **2814 Fredericksburg Road
> San Antonio, TX 78201
> 210-732-0191
> www.tiptopcafe.com**

Third-generation owner Linda started running the place when her father retired in 1981. She says she knows it's a business, but it's more family than anything. Nothing changes, from the recipes to the decor; they just like doing it the way they've been doing it for seventy years.

There's chicken and dumplings, chicken-fried steak, pork ribs, corn casserole, mashed potatoes, and a whole lot more. Chef Troy Wells does a pork roast that is out-of-this-world tender, with a rich brown gravy. It puts the shamalama in ding dong. Ask me in a year if that's what we make in my house for Christmas.

And they are still cutting their own steaks and grinding their own beef for burgers and the homemade chili on their enchiladas—which are considered comfort food in this town. The chili starts with the ground beef, then chopped onion, salt, black pepper, beef base, cumin, and garlic powder. It all cooks down for about two hours on low. Then they add the chili powder and tomato sauce and some water and let it simmer a bit. Then they drop two red corn tortillas in hot oil for a second to soften them up, put shredded Monterey Jack cheese in them, ladle on a little chili, and add some shredded American cheese. I wouldn't walk in here and expect an enchilada like that. That's like Grandma's-blanket-next-to-a-fire comfort.

They also make about two hundred fifty pounds of onion rings a day, between ten AM and closing time. The chicken-fried steak is popular, but so are the shrimp. They get a flour coating, then an egg wash with egg, salt, and milk; then they get dipped in fresh cracker crumbs. Into the fryer, and out come some nice, big, succulent, buttery shrimp—the definition of a fried shrimp dinner.

There's a lot of love going into the food here, and you'll never leave hungry.

Roasted Pork Butt with Gravy

ADAPTED FROM A RECIPE COURTESY OF DEWESE'S TIP TOP CAFÉ

This pork roast could cure all ailments.

6 TO 8 SERVING

Marinade

2 tablespoons light brown sugar

2 teaspoons ground ginger

2 teaspoons garlic powder

2 teaspoons dried mustard

2 teaspoons celery salt

½ cup vegetable oil

¼ cup soy sauce

2 teaspoons cider vinegar

2 teaspoons liquid smoke

2 teaspoons Worcestershire sauce

Pork Roast

1 (5- to 6-pound) bone-in Boston butt (pork butt)

Freshly ground black pepper

2 tablespoons dried rosemary

1 tablespoon unsalted butter

1 tablespoon all-purpose flour

Salt and freshly ground black pepper

1. For the marinade: Mix the sugar, ginger, garlic powder, mustard, and celery salt together in a large nonreactive bowl. Then whisk in the oil, soy, vinegar, liquid smoke, and Worcestershire.

2. For the pork roast: Put the pork in the marinade and turn to coat evenly. Cover and refrigerate for 8 hours or overnight.

3. Position a rack in the middle of the oven and preheat to 350°F. Put the pork roast in a roasting pan, season generously with black pepper, and scatter the rosemary over the meat. Roast the pork, uncovered, until the meat starts to fall off the bone, 3½ to 4 hours. Transfer the roast to a carving board and let rest for 20 minutes before slicing. (Reserve the roasting pan.)

4. To make the gravy, pour the pan drippings from the roast into a fat separator and discard the excess fat. Melt the butter in a medium saucepan over medium heat. Add the flour and cook, stirring for 1 minute, to make a paste (or roux). Place the roasting pan over two burners on medium-high heat. Add 1½ cups water to the pan and scrape up any brown bits clinging to the bottom of the pan. Let the liquid come to a simmer, and then strain into the saucepan with the roux. Whisk the gravy and bring to a boil; add the reserved pan drippings. Simmer the gravy until thickened and season to taste with salt and pepper.

5. Slice the pork and serve with the gravy.

Bobby's Hawaiian Style Restaurant

EST. 2007 ★ SWING BY FOR A REAL-DEAL LUAU

Located just outside Seattle, this is a place as true to its family origins in music as it is in food. It's a nonstop party here, and owner Bobby Nakihei's strumming the strings and manning the grill to the tune of everything he grew up with in Hawaii, from the pork you get at a luau, to island-style barbecue and salt-cured salmon.

★ TRACK IT DOWN ★

**1011 Hewitt Avenue West
Everett, WA 98201
425-259-1338
www.bobbyshawaiianstyle
restaurant.com**

Bobby and his wife, Diana, moved to Washington State in 1989. He kept cooking as a hobby, then decided to take a chance. Here in downtown Everett, they've got a constant crowd of transplanted islanders and appreciative locals. I found out about this place from a viewer e-mail: Vincent Abella said Bobby's food is the bomb, and people ought to know about it.

The most famous Hawaiian dish of all—in fact, Bobby says it's not a luau without one—is Kalua Pig. Bobby starts with pork butt, which he seasons with Hawaiian salt (like what dries on the rocks after waves crash, says Bobby). Then he places a banana leaf in the bottom of a deep pan. (Wait, a banana leaf? And bananas is good.) The pork goes on top of the leaf, it's covered by another leaf, and then the pan is sealed with aluminum foil. It cooks for eight to ten hours at 250°F, and it renders down because of the fat and the moisture. It just falls apart—very tender, like pulled pork without the smoke. You get a hint of the banana leaf, too.

Diana says people are surprised by the simplicity of preparing Hawaiian food. Like traditional Lomi Lomi Salmon, which is kind of like a raw salmon ceviche, or Lau Lau, which is cubed pork wrapped in edible taro leaf and steamed in a pressure cooker. Then there's Spam Musubi. See, during World War Two, Spam was the cheapest item in the grocery in Hawaii. So a musubi is half sushi and half Spam. Bobby flash-fries a couple slices of Spam, then takes it over to the grill, where he brushes on his secret sauce while it cooks. (It smelled great, like ginger, honey, and soy.) He then places some rice on sheets of nori (seaweed), securely sandwiching the Spam between two little bricks of rice before closing the wrap—so it's open on two ends like sushi. That's like a Hawaiian hamburger.

For some, it's a taste of home; for others, it's a different kind of home cooking. And yes, they made me do the hula. (Stop laughing.)

Guess who got stuck with the kazoo?

Lomi Lomi Salmon

ADAPTED FROM A RECIPE COURTESY OF BOBBY NAKIHEI OF BOBBY'S HAWAIIAN STYLE RESTAURANT

Lomi lomi means "to mix." This is kind of like a salsa without the sauce, and it's tasty. Be sure to soak the salted salmon the night before you plan to make this dish.

6 SERVINGS

1 cup diced salted salmon

5 medium tomatoes, diced

1 medium onion, diced

¼ cup thinly sliced green onions, green parts only

Sea salt

1 cup crushed ice

1. In a large bowl, cover the salted salmon with water and soak overnight in the fridge.

2. Drain and rinse the salmon. In a large bowl, add the salmon, tomatoes, onion, and green onions and mix well. Add sea salt to taste. Chill. Just before serving, add the crushed ice.

COOK'S NOTE: If unsalted salmon is used, rub it with sea salt or rock salt and let stand overnight in the fridge before using.

A 100% kalua pig smile . . .

. . . that makes you go *crazy*!

Mike's Chili Parlor

EST. 1922 ★ CHILI PARLOR, PLAIN AND SIMPLE

★ TRACK IT DOWN ★

**1447 NW Ballard Way
Seattle, WA 98107
206-782-2808
www.mikeschiliparlor.com**

Seattle is known for its killer food, and there's this joint you've got to check out here in Ballard—in an industrial park just across the bridge from downtown. This third-generation father-and-son team runs a one-of-a-kind parlor filled with local flavor.

Phil Semandiris and his son Mike take their chili very seriously. "I love it in chili burgers, chili dogs. I love my chili." And so do the locals. As one says, "Life is short, what better way to spend a lot of it." It's got a little kick, and as one regular puts it, it defines chili. And chili defines everything at this place. You see, Mike's Chili Parlor is true to its name: you have chili on whatever you order, from chili fries to dogs and burgers. Take a look at the menu on the wall. The grilled cheese is $54.25. Why? Mike says you really, really have to want a grilled cheese. Okay, it's a joke, but trust me—it ain't the grilled cheese they're coming for.

What's most out-of-control are the combo plates, like the burger that has a tower of chili, beans, thinly grated cheese (which melts nicely), onions, hot peppers . . . whew. That burger's in it to win it. And check out the chili pasta: a big bowl of spaghetti with chili, cheese, onions, and jalapeños. I mean, I'm Italian and I know a few things about pasta, and this flies. I loved the jalapeño nuggets mixed in there, a great kicker.

The recipe's been a closely guarded family secret for more than eighty-five years. It's not written down anywhere. Instead it's been passed down from Mike's great-grandfather, also named Mike. His grandfather

GUY ASIDE

What a bunch of characters these guys are. Really good chili on spaghetti, and a funky old stove they were cooking on. Some people were building a big mall behind them and they were offered a big bunch of money to move, but they held out, kept getting offered money, and held out. They never caved. So I think the place was built around them. Old school.

and great-grandfather came from Greece, and like a lot of Greeks, he says, they started working in a restaurant. Great-grandpa Mike came up with this great chili recipe and decided he wanted to open his own restaurant. When Phil was twenty-one, he and his dad took the place over, then in '66 Phil started running the place on his own. Twenty years later, Mike jumped into the pot. And they're proud to tell you, they've changed virtually nothing.

As Mike points out, "You know, you can't create a place like this; it has to happen over time."

The daily meeting of the Seattle Chili Club.

TOP: **Bruthas of the chili.**

MIDDLE: **It's not often you see my mouth closed!**

BOTTOM: **My twin— a great dude!**

The Non-Recipe for Mike's Chili Parlor Chili

UNAUTHORIZED, COURTESY OF THE SEMANDIRIS FAMILY OF MIKE'S CHILI PARLOR

SERVES A CROWD

Beef stock

White onions, chopped

Garlic, chopped

Ground meat

Spice mixture that includes chili powder and oregano

1. There's no "filler" here, as Mike calls it, no beans mixed into the meat, although they serve the chili over beans. True chili is meat only.

2. So, it starts with a big pot of beef stock, chopped white onions, and garlic. Not sautéed, just thrown into the pool.

3. Next comes the meat, and you mix it until it all breaks down. It's quite a workout. This is called "making the sauce."

4. After several hours of simmering, the sauce is finally ready for the big bag of spices. I swear, there are like eighty-five different spices going on there. There's got to be some chili powder, some oregano . . . Phil had no intention of telling me. But that was more than he'd ever done for anybody else.

5. It simmers just a little while longer.

6. Then watch out; it's addictive.

Voula's Offshore Café

EST. 1955, RE-EST. 1984 ★ YOUR GREEK FAMILY BY THE WATERFRONT

Normally when you think about entertainment while you're eating, well, you might think of a Vegas dinner show. But let's say you're in Seattle, down by the waterfront. Here you'll find an entertaining crew serving up stuffed grape leaves, smoked pork Benedict, and some killer homemade blueberry pie.

★ TRACK IT DOWN ★

**658 NE Northlake Way
Seattle, WA 98105
206-634-0183
www.voulasoffshore.com**

Owner Voula Vlahos gave me a big hug when I came in, saying, "I always love handsome men, baby." ('Course that sold me already.) To Voula, every customer is family. She has all her customers' kids' photos plastered on the wall. She says you have to hug your customers; you have to love them. I ask her where she got this philosophy of restaurants. She says, "This is Greek philosophy."

And that philosophy includes tons of homemade food, from egg scrambles filled with meat and cheese to pie. As one regular puts it, "It's just a great restaurant run by a great family." On the line, you'll find her sons, Nikos and Sikey, and Bryan Albright—who, after working alongside these guys for the past fifteen years, is one of the family, too.

GUY ASIDE

I totally dig this place. They've become like family. These guys have been to barbecue competitions with me, come down for my birthday, all kinds of events. You know, so much more comes out of this stuff: they're lifelong friends.

Voula bought the place to help put Sikey through college. Sikey worked there through school and mastered the menu that Voula put together. Everything Voula has, from the basic, like meatloaf, to the bizarre, like a Chinese pancake, is somethin' special. The Chinese pancake came about because people order ham, eggs, and pancakes—so they just put it all together in one big pancake. Hands-down that was the weirdest thing I've ever seen for breakfast, but it works.

Also weird: check out what's in their parking lot. They're smoking fresh Pacific salmon for their Smoky the Salmon scramble. Served over hash browns, it's nice and light and a huge seller. Then it's back to the parking lot to smoke a pork butt for a smoked pork–chipotle eggs Benedict. Voula also does traditional Greek favorites like her mother's recipe for hand-rolled, beef- and rice-filled grape leaves called dolmades. Her blueberry pie is made from actual never-been-frozen berries—no filler here.

The boys do all they can to do everything the way Mom started it. Technically, she's not even here anymore. She recently retired, but she just can't stay away. After all, the name of the place is Voula's.

Two of the coolest dudes I've ever met, Nikos and Sikey . . . now, get off my ride! Ha ha ha.

Hobo

ADAPTED FROM A RECIPE COURTESY OF SIKEY VLAHOS OF VOULA'S OFFSHORE CAFÉ

So I see a plate of something go by and I ask Nikos what it is, and he says a Greek Hobo. I say no, I didn't mean your brother . . . But seriously, it looked good. They start with a sauté of onions, mushrooms, Greek sausage (which is spiced like gyro meat), and a couple eggs mixed together, then they fresh-grate Cheddar over the top. That's a party and totally unique. All kinds of props on this; here's the basic version.

4 SERVINGS

12 ounces country-style sausage, bulk or removed from casing

½ cup chopped yellow onion

½ cup sliced fresh mushrooms

¼ cup vegetable oil

3 cups fresh shredded hash brown potatoes

6 large eggs, lightly beaten

1 cup shredded Cheddar cheese

The griddle actually speaks to Nikos . . . or so he thinks!

1. Brown the sausage meat in a large skillet over medium-high heat. (Drain the excess fat, if desired.) Add the onion and mushrooms and cook until tender. Transfer the mixture to a bowl.

2. Add the oil to the skillet; when hot, add the hash browns and press evenly into the skillet. Cook over medium-high heat until golden brown on one side. Stir in the eggs and the sausage mixture and scramble everything together, cooking to the desired consistency. Then scatter the cheese over the top. Cover with a lid and continue to cook until the cheese melts. Serve.

Bryan can just sense them staring him down.

Recipe Index

List of Restaurants

Here's a list of all the terrific restaurants that have been shown on Diners, Drive-ins and Dives. *The restaurants in blue are featured in this book. But you gotta visit 'em all!*

❏ **A1 DINER**
3 Bridge Street
Gardiner, ME 04345
(207) 582-4804
www.a1diner.com/menus

❏ **ALPINE STEAKHOUSE**
4520 S. Tamiami Trail
Sarasota, FL 34231
(941) 921-3798
(941) 922-3797
www.alpinesteak.com

❏ **AL'S BREAKFAST**
413 14th Avenue, SE
Minneapolis, MN 55414
(612) 331-9991

❏ **AUNT LENA'S CREAMERY**
4040 S. Arizona Avenue
Chandler, AZ 85248
(480) 802-1100
www.auntlena.net

❏ **BABY BLUES BAR-B-Q**
444 Lincoln Boulevard
Venice, CA 90291
(310) 396-7675
www.babybluesvenice.com

❏ **BARBEQUE KING DRIVE-IN**
2900 Wilkinson Boulevard
Charlotte, NC 28208
(704) 399-8344

❏ **BAYWAY DINER**
2019 S. Wood Avenue
Linden, NJ 07036
(908) 862-3207
www.baywaydiner.org

❏ **BBQ SHACK**
705 N. Pearl Street
Paola, KS 66071
(913) 294-5908
www.thebbqshack.com

❏ **BEACON DRIVE-IN**
255 John B. White Boulevard
Spartanburg, SC 29306
(864) 585-9387
www.beacondrivein.com

❏ **BENNY'S SEAFOOD**
2500 SW 107th Avenue
South Miami, FL 33165
(305) 227-1232

❏ **BIG STAR DINER**
305 Madison Avenue North
Bainbridge Island, WA 98110
(206) 842-5786

❏ **BLUE MOON CAFÉ**
1621 Aliceanna Street
Baltimore, MD 21321
(410) 522-3940

❏ **BOBBY'S HAWAIIAN STYLE RESTAURANT**
1011 Hewitt Avenue West
Everett, WA 98201
(425) 259-1388
www.bobbyshawaiian
    stylerestaurant.com

❏ **BOBO DRIVE-IN**
2300 SW 10th Street
Topeka, KS 66604
(785) 234-4511

❏ **BRINT'S DINER**
4834 E. Lincoln Street
Wichita, KS 67218
(316) 684-0290

❏ **BROWNSTONE DINER AND PANCAKE FACTORY**
426 Jersey Avenue
Jersey City, NJ 07302
(201) 433-0471
www.brownstonediner.com

❏ **BYWAYS CAFÉ**
1212 NW Gilsan Street
Portland, OR 97209
(503) 221-0011
www.bywayscafe.com

❏ **CAFÉ ON THE ROUTE**
1101 Military Avenue
Baxter Springs, KS 66713
(620) 856-5646
www.cafeontheroute.com

❏ **CENTRAL CITY CAFÉ**
529 14th Street West
Huntington, WV 25704
(304) 522-6142

❏ **CHAP'S PIT BEEF**
5801 Pulaski Highway
Baltimore, MD 21205
(410) 483-2379
www.chapspitbeef.com

❏ **CHARLIE PARKER'S**
700 North Street
Springfield, IL 62704
(217) 241-2104
(217) 522-8291

❏ **CHARLIE'S**
32 W. Main Street
Spencer, MA 01562
(508) 885-4033

❏ **CHINO BANDIDO**
15414 N. 19th Avenue, Suite K
Phoenix, AZ 85023
(602) 375-3639
www.chinobandido.com

❏ **THE COFFEE CUP**
512 Nevada Way
Boulder City, NV 89005
(702) 294-0517
www.worldfamouscoffeecup
    .com

COZY CORNER
745 N. Parkway
Memphis, TN 38105
(901) 527-9158
www.cozycornerbbq.com

❏ **CREOLE CREAMERY**
4924 Prytania Street
New Orleans, LA 70115
(504) 894-8680
www.creolecreamery.com

❏ **DADDYPOPS DINER**
232 N. York Road
Hatboro, PA 19040
(215) 675-9717

❏ **DARI-ETTE DRIVE-IN**
1440 Minnehaha Avenue East
St. Paul, MN 55106
(651) 776-3470

❏ **DEWESE'S TIP TOP CAFÉ**
2814 Fredericksburg Road
San Antonio, TX 78201
(210) 732-0191
www.tiptopcafe.com

❏ **THE DINING CAR**
8826 Frankford Avenue
Philadelphia, PA 19136
(215) 338-5113
www.thediningcar.com

❏ **DOT'S BACK INN**
4030 Macarthur Avenue
Richmond, VA 23227
(804) 266-3167

❏ **DOUMAR'S**
1919 Monticello Avenue
Norfolk, VA 23517
(757) 627-4163
www.doumars.com

❏ **DUARTE'S TAVERN**
202 Stage Road
Pescadero, CA 94060
(650) 879-0464
www.duartestavern.com

❏ **EL INDIO MEXICAN RESTAURANT**
3695 India Street
San Diego, CA 92103
(619) 299-0333
www.el-indio.com

❏ **11TH STREET DINER**
1065 Washington Avenue
Miami Beach, FL 33139
(305) 354-6373

❏ **EMMA JEAN'S HOLLAND BURGER CAFÉ**
17143 D Street on Route 66
Victorville, CA 92394
(760) 243-9938

❏ **EVELYN'S DRIVE-IN**
2335 Main Road (Route 77)
Tiverton, RI 02878
(401) 624-3100
www.evelynsdrivein.com

❏ **EVEREADY DINER**
4189 Albany Post Road
(Route 9 North)
Hyde Park, NY 12538
(845) 229-8100
www.theevereadydiner.com

❏ **THE FLY TRAP**
22950 Woodward Avenue
Ferndale, MI 48220
(248) 399-5150
www.theflytrapferndale.com

❏ **FOUR KEGS SPORTS PUB**
267 N. Jones Boulevard
Las Vegas, NV 89107
(702) 870-0255
www.fourkegs.com

❏ **FRANKS DINER**
508 58th Street
Kenosha, WI 53140
(262) 657-1017
www.franksdinerkenosha.com

❏ **THE FROSTED MUG**
11541 South Pulaski Road
Alsip, IL 60803
(708) 371-3383
www.thefrostedmug.com

❏ **GAFFEY STREET DINER**
247 N. Gaffey Street
San Pedro, CA 90731
(310) 548-6964
www.gaffeystreetdiner.com

❏ **GALEWOOD COOKSHACK**
Various locations
Chicago, IL
(773) 470-8334
www.galewoodcookshack
   .com

❏ **GRAMPA'S BAKERY AND RESTAURANT**
17 SW First Street
Dania Beach, FL 33004
(954) 923-2163
www.grampasbakery.com

❏ **GRUBSTAKE**
1525 Pine Street
San Francisco, CA 94109
(415) 673-8268
www.sfgrubstake.com

❏ **HACKNEY'S ON HARMS**
1241 Harms Road
Glenview, IL 60025
(847) 724-5577
www.hackneys.net

❏ **HANK'S CREEKSIDE RESTAURANT**
2800 4th Street
Santa Rosa, CA 95405
(707) 575-8839
www.sterba.com/sro/creek
   side/wine.html

❏ **HAROLD'S RESTAURANT**
602 N. Limestone Street
Gaffney, SC 29340
(864) 489-9153
www.haroldsrestaurant.com

❏ **HIGHSTOWN DINER**
151 Mercer Street
Highstown, NJ 08520
(609) 443-4600

❏ **HILLBILLY HOT DOGS**
6591 Ohio River Road
Lesage, WV 25537
(304) 762-2458
www.hillbillyhotdogs.com

❏ **HODAD'S**
5010 Newport Avenue
Ocean Beach, CA 92107
(619) 224-4623

❏ **HULLABALOO DINER**
15045 F.M. 2154
Wellborn, TX 77883
(979) 690-3002
www.hullabaloodiner.com

❏ **IRON BARLEY**
5510 Virginia Avenue
St. Louis, MO 63111
(314) 351-4500
www.ironbarley.com

❏ **JAY BEE'S**
15911 Avalon Boulevard
Gardena, CA 90247
(310) 532-1064
www.jaybeesbbq.com

❏ **JEFFERSON DINER**
5 Bowling Green Parkway
Lake Hopatcong, NJ 07849
(973) 663-0233
www.jeffersondiner.com

❏ **JOE'S CABLE CAR**
4320 Mission Street
San Francisco, CA 94112
(415) 334-6699
www.joescablecar.com

❏ **JOE'S FARM GRILL**
3000 E. Ray Road
Gilbert, AZ 85296
(480) 563-4745
www.joesfarmgrill.com

JOE'S GIZZARD CITY
120 W. Main Street
Potterville, MI 48876
(517) 645-2120
www.gizzardcity.com

J.T. FARNHAM'S
88 Eastern Avenue
(Route 133)
South Essex, MA 01929
(978) 768-6643

KEEGAN'S SEAFOOD GRILLE
1519 Gulf Boulevard
Indian Rocks Beach, FL 33785
(727) 596-2477
www.keegansseafood.com

KELLY'S DINER
674 Broadway
Somerville, MA 02144
(617) 623-8102

KRAZY JIM'S
551 S. Division Street
Ann Arbor, MI 48104
(734) 663-4590
www.blimpyburger.com

LEONARD'S
5465 Fox Plaza Drive
Memphis, TN 38115
(901) 360-1963
www.leonardsbarbecue.com

LEO'S BBQ
3631 N. Kelley Avenue
Oklahoma City, OK 73111
(405) 424-5367

LITTLE TEA SHOP
69 Monroe Avenue
Memphis, TN 38103
(901) 525-6000

LOS TAPATIOS
1141 Old Bayshore Highway
San Jose, CA 95112
(408) 729-6199

LOUIE MUELLER BARBECUE
206 W. Second Street
Taylor, TX 76574
(512) 352-6206
www.louiemuellerbarbecue.com

MAC AND ERNIE'S ROADSIDE EATERY
Williams Creek Depot FM 470
Tarpley, TX 78883
(830) 562-3250
www.macandernies.com

MAD GREEK'S DINER
72112 Baker Boulevard
Baker, CA 92309
(760) 733-4354

MAMA'S 39TH STREET DINER
3906 Waddell Street
Kansas City, MO 64111
(816) 531-6422

MARIA'S TACO XPRESS
2529 S. Lamar Boulevard
Austin, TX 78704
(512) 444-0261
www.tacoxpress.com

MARIETTA DINER
306 Cobb Parkway North
Marietta, GA 30062
(770) 423-9390
www.mariettadiner.net

MARLOWE'S RIBS
4381 Elvis Presley Boulevard
Memphis, TN 38116
(901) 332-4159
www.marlowesmemphis.com

MATTHEW'S CAFETERIA
2299 Main Street
Tucker, GA 30084
(770) 939-2357
www.matthewscafeteria.com

MATT'S BIG BREAKFAST
801 N. 1st Street
Phoenix, AZ 85004
(602) 254-1074

MIKE'S CHILI PARLOR
1447 NW Ballard Way
Seattle, WA 98107
(206) 782-2808
www.mikeschiliparlor.com

MIKE'S CITY DINER
1714 Washington Street
Boston, MA 02118
(617) 267-9393

MOGRIDDER'S
565 Hunts Point Avenue
Bronx, NY 10474
(718) 991-3046
www.mogridder.com

MONTE CARLO STEAKHOUSE
3916 Central SW
Albuquerque, NM 87105
(505) 836-9886

MUSTACHE BILL'S DINER
8th Avenue and Broadway Street
Barnegat Light, NJ 08005
(609) 494-0155

NADINE'S
10 S. 27th Street
Pittsburgh, PA 19203
(412) 481-1793

THE NOOK
492 Hamline Avenue South
St. Paul, MN 55116
(651) 698-4347

THE ORIGINAL FALAFEL'S DRIVE-IN
2301 Stevens Creek Boulevard
San Jose, CA 95128
(408) 294-7886
www.falafelsdrivein.com

PANINI PETE'S
42½ South Section Street
Fairhope, AL 36532
(251) 929-0122
www.paninipetes.com

PARADISE PUP
1724 S. River Road
Des Plaines, IL 60018
(847) 699-8590

PATRICK'S ROADHOUSE
106 Entrada Drive
Los Angeles, CA 90402
(310) 459-4544
www.patricksroadhouse.info

PENGUIN DRIVE-IN
1921 Commonwealth Avenue
Charlotte, NC 28205
(704) 375-6959
www.penguindrivein.com

PIZZA PALACE
3132 E. Magnolia Avenue
Knoxville, TN 37914
(865) 524-4388
www.visitpizzapalace.com

PSYCHO SUZI'S
2519 Marshall Street NE
Minneapolis, MN 55418
(612) 788-9069
www.psychosuzis.com

RAMONA CAFÉ
628 Main Street
Ramona, CA 92605
(760) 789-8656
www.ramonacafe.com

❑ **RED ARROW DINER**
61 Lowell Street
Manchester, NH 03101
(603) 626-1118
www.redarrowdiner.com

❑ **THE RITZ**
72 E. Mount Pleasant Avenue
Livingston, NJ 07039
(973) 533-1213

❑ **RIVERSHACK TAVERN**
3449 River Road
Jefferson, LA 70121
(504) 834-4938
www.therivershacktavern.com

❑ **ROBERTO'S**
675 W. Union Hills Drive
Phoenix, AZ 85027
(602) 439-7279

❑ **THE ROCK CAFÉ**
114 Main Street
Stroud, OK 74079
(918) 968-3990

❑ **ROSIE'S DINER**
4500 14 Mile Road
Rockford, MI 49341
(616) 866-3663
www.rosiesdiner.com

❑ **RUSSIAN RIVER PUB**
11829 River Road
Forestville, CA 95436
(707) 887-7932

❑ **SCHOONER OR LATER**
241 N. Marina Drive
Long Beach, CA 90803
(562) 708-6946

❑ **SCULLY'S TAVERN**
9809 Sunset Drive
Miami, FL 33173
(305) 271-7404
www.scullystavern.net

❑ **SILK CITY PHILLY**
435 Spring Garden Street
Philadelphia, PA 19123
(215) 592-8838
www.silkcityphilly.com

❑ **THE SKYLARK FINE DINING AND LOUNGE**
Route 1 and Wooding Avenue
Edison, NJ 08817
(732) 777-7878
www.skylarkdiner.com

❑ **SMOKEY VALLEY TRUCK STOP**
40 Bond Court
Olive Hill, KY 41164
(606) 286-5001

❑ **SMOQUE**
3800 N. Pulaski Road
Chicago, IL 60641
(773) 545-7427
www.smoquebbq.com

❑ **SOUTH SIDE SODA SHOP AND DINER**
1122 South Main Street
Goshen, IN 46526
(574) 534-3790
www.southsidesodashopdiner
.com

❑ **SQUEEZE INN**
7918 Fruitridge Road
Sacramento, CA 95820
(916) 386-8599

❑ **STUDIO DINER**
4701 Ruffin Road
San Diego, CA 92123
(858) 715-6400
www.studiodiner.com

❑ **SWEETIE PIE'S**
4270 Manchester Avenue
St. Louis, MO 63110
(314) 371-0304

❑ **TAYLOR'S AUTOMATIC REFRESHER**
933 Main Street
St. Helena, CA 94574
(707) 963-3486
www.taylorsrefresher.com

❑ **TECOLOTE CAFÉ**
1203 Cerrillos Road
Santa Fe, NM 87505
(505) 988-1362
www.tecolotecafe.com

❑ **TED PETERS**
1350 Pasadena Avenue
South Pasadena, FL 33707
(727) 381-7931

❑ **THEE PITTS AGAIN**
5558 W. Bel Road
Glendale, AZ 85308
(602) 996-7488
www.theepittsagain.com

❑ **TICK TOCK DINER**
281 Allwood Road
Clifton, NJ 07012
(973) 777-0511
www.ticktockdiner.com

❑ **TOM'S BAR-B-Q**
4087 Getwell Road
Memphis, TN 38118
(901) 365-6690
www.tomsbarbq.com

❑ **TRIPLE XXX FAMILY RESTAURANT**
2 N. Salisbury Street
West Lafayette, IN 47906
(765) 743-5373
www.triplexxxfamily
restaurant.com

❑ **VILLAGE CAFÉ**
1001 W. Grace Street
Richmond, VA 23220
(804) 353-8204
www.villagecafeonline.com

❑ **VIRGINIA DINER**
322 W. Main Street
Wakefield, VA 23888
(888) 823-4637
www.vadiner.com

❑ **VOULA'S OFFSHORE CAFÉ**
658 NE Northlake Way
Seattle, WA 98105
(206) 634-0183
www.voulasoffshore.com

❑ **WHITE MANNA**
358 River Street
Hackensack, NJ 07601
(201) 342-0914

❑ **WHITE PALACE GRILL**
1159 S. Canal Street
Chicago, IL 60607
(312) 939-7167

❑ **WILLIE BIRD'S**
1150 Santa Rosa Avenue
Santa Rosa, CA 95404
(707) 542-0861
www.williebirdsrestaurant
.com

❑ **YJ'S SNACK BAR**
128 W. 18th Street
Kansas City, MO 64108
(816) 472-5533